It's You Against You

*40 Principles to Help You Master Life
and Win at Being You*

It's You Against You: 40 Principles to Help You Master Life and Win at Being You

Book design by:
Rick Chappell

Printed in the United States of America

It's You Against You: 40 Principles to Help You Master Life and Win at Being You
Tracey Knight

1. Title 2. Author 3. Self-Help

ISBN 13: 978-1-7339437-0-3

It's You Against You

40 Principles to Help You Master Life
and Win at Being You

I AM
TRACEY KNIGHT.COM

Contents

Self-Care Principles

TOOLS

Preface

WELCOME MESSAGE FROM COACH TRACEY

Welcome to ***It's You Against You: 40 Principles to Help You Master Life and Win at Being You,*** the first of several experiences in the Master Your Life series. I want to congratulate you on having the courage to accept this challenge, which has been created to support you in becoming the next version of yourself. Although you will be blocking off 40 days to focus on elevating your consciousness in a few key areas, it is important to understand that this will be lifelong work. We never complete this quest. We simply climb to the next level and begin the self-mastery journey again from our new vantage point. That may be disconcerting for some people; I know it was for me! But once I realized that my disappointment was rooted in impatience and perfectionism, I could see that this too was an area that required attention and love. What I have grown to realize is that "*becoming me*" is a process that will either be enjoyed or despised over the course of my time on this earth. The decision is mine. If I choose to detest it (and myself), I will make every experience difficult and painful. If I choose to appreciate the process and "all" that it offers, life will be a wonderous experience. You will have to make that decision too. The question is, how do you make every experience joyous when there are so many things that feel scary, laborious, awkward and sometimes just plain awful? It might be helpful if you first understand what it means to "*win at being you*" as well as the process you'll go through to become a more powerful version of yourself.

This may sound odd, but most of us have been conditioned to be anything but ourselves. From the time we enter school (and often long before then) we are conditioned to fit into social norms. We are taught to think, walk, talk, learn, behave, dress, play and present ourselves in ways that are acceptable to others. Don Miguel Ruiz, author of the "Four Agreements," calls this *domestication*. If we conform, we are rewarded with acceptance, approval, accolades and the title of being a "good" girl or boy. If we fail to comply and operate outside of how our family, religious institutions, schools, friends, media, et cetera think we should be, we are deemed a "bad" girl or boy and punished in a variety of ways, including suspension of privileges, denial of affection or approval, being isolated or even subjected to verbal or physical reprimands. Sometimes this conditioning is so subtle we barely notice it; however, it happens so frequently throughout childhood and as we become adults that we begin to place great value on what others want and think and use it as a guidepost for our actions. We begin to believe that our way of being is not the "right way," thus, we ignore and sometimes forget who we are and what we need. We sabotage our success and set aside our heart's desires just to fit in and seem "normal."

None of this, however, changes one essential truth: you take you wherever you go. You cannot change who you truly are - authentically. It's law! Despite your best efforts to assimilate, there is and will always be some part of you that feels a little out-of-sorts or uncomfortable. You may also notice that when trying to bring goals to fruition you fall short, don't follow through, or feel exhausted by the effort. The only way to squelch this feeling is to become comfortable being you. To *win at being you* will require that you deprogram much of what you have been conditioned to think and do for the last twenty, thirty or forty-plus years. You see, what most people want in life is to be happy, safe and free. But these qualities are only available when you discover your truth and surrender the need for acceptance and validation. You know true happiness when you realize just how powerful you are, just by being yourself. You will feel free when you stop trying to control outcomes. You will feel safe when you replace dishonesty and deception with a newfound loyalty and responsibility for yourself.

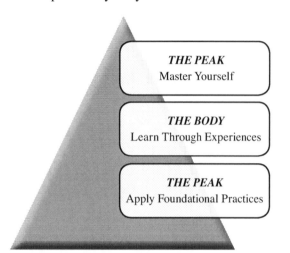

THE PEAK
Master Yourself

THE BODY
Learn Through Experiences

THE PEAK
Apply Foundational Practices

As for the process, I have found it is best illustrated by the depiction of a pyramid. A pyramid is constructed on a wide base in order to hold the weight and height of the ascending layers. Most people focus on the awe-inspiring peak as it personifies the pinnacle of success. However, they fail to acknowledge the body of the pyramid (i.e. everything between the point and the base) that has graduated layers and represents the bulk of the structure. It is safe to assume that it was a process to go from the base to the top of the pyramid, much like when we are working to master some aspect of our life. To win at being you, you must learn to love yourself unconditionally. This requires you to solidify your base through a set of foundational practices that are explained in the next section. Most of your growth, however, will come from the ongoing cycle of unearthing and correcting beliefs and habits that are self-sabotaging and judgmental. Using the 40 principles of self-mastery and self-care covered in this book will help you discover where these disruptive viewpoints and behaviors are hidden. Each time you participate in this 40-Day Journey, you will immerse yourself in a self-selected lesson that will be reinforced in your daily activities ("the school of life"). Much like formal education, life's lessons are designed to build one on top of the other to encourage progressive growth. The more committed you are and the more consistently you practice and integrate with each principle, the stronger and more confident you will become. As your confidence increases, so will your ability to resiliently cope with setbacks and disappointments. While the experiences at each level may increase in intensity, you will find that you have been readied by, and are building upon, your successes of the prior stages. You will no longer want to quit on yourself, and that can only lead to success. That said, it is your mindset that will be your greatest asset, your biggest obstacle, and the determining factor in how swiftly and effortlessly you move. At the end of the day, "It's You, Against You." The pinnacle of achievement is not the finish line or desired attainment, that's just the icing on the proverbial cake. Rather, it is the point in the process when you intentionally seek out and conquer the fears that have kept you paralyzed and mediocre - all while utilizing, managing and cherishing the uniqueness of you. This is true power. This is self-mastery!

Why forty principles and forty days? For the millennia, the number forty has signified trials and transformation, from Moses' forty days on the mount to forty days and forty nights Jesus fasted in the desert. In numerology, 40 reduces to the #4, which holds the energy of destiny and hard work; the Angel Number 40 is a message from our angels, reminding us that we're safe, loved, protected and supported. Finally, a square has four equal sides, meaning it has no weak points. It is solid and enduring. We can surmise from the above references that 40 means we are safe, love and have unwavering support in our quest to confront and heal the pieces of ourselves that are hidden, fragile and scared.

Remember though, the initial 40 days is designed to focus your mind and jumpstart the process. You cannot put a time limit on mastering a particular principle. There are some areas that will be easy to address, and you will likely see rapid growth. Other matters are deeply rooted and will take more time. Consistency, determination and patience with yourself are the keys to success. I promise, if you commit to this work, you will take back your power, transform and win at your own life.

HOW TO USE THIS BOOK

Apply the Foundational Practices

To fortify the base of your pyramid, you will need to A.R.M. yourself with three foundational practices – Self-**A**wareness, Self-**R**esponsibility and Self-**M**anagement. These powerful skills and tools are the driving force behind self-mastery and must be constantly used when completing any 40-Day Journey, and in *all* your daily affairs.

1.   **A**wareness:

Self-awareness is the practice of revealing, acknowledging and loving all aspects of your being. This will require you to be vulnerable and use personal integrity in every aspect of your life, regardless of the circumstances. Using personal integrity means learning how to trust and respect yourself like never before. The reason our self-confidence vacillates between strength and fragility is because we don't always tell or honor our truth. Most of us stifle how we feel or modify what we think because we want to avoid conflict and/or be liked by others. We "people please" to our own demise. Years of dishonoring our truth diminishes our ability to fully respect and trust ourselves to stand up for what we want or need. As you practice acknowledging your truth, you may feel uncomfortable and uncertain. This is normal. You are stripping away lies and shattering the false ideas about your persona. This level of transparency may make you feel vulnerable, but it is in this space that your authentic self is revealed. Contrary to popular belief, vulnerability is not weakness, but the ultimate showing of strength. The more you accept the truth of who you are, the greater your confidence. The more confidence you have the more powerful you will become.

Your Homework:

- ✓ Be honest and honor your truth at all times.

- ✓ Accept yourself, others and circumstances just as they are in this moment but recognize that you have the power to change "you." When you shift, so does everything else.

- ✓ When you feel vulnerable, lean in rather than shutting down, fleeing or isolating yourself. Use these moments as an opportunity to learn your triggers, support yourself and build your faith with Spirit. Most importantly, follow your intuitive guidance.

2.   **R**esponsibility:

Self-responsibility is the practice of taking 100% ownership of everything that happens in your life. This requires an understanding of your innate power to choose and manifest what you want. Of the three Foundational Practices, this may initially feel like the most difficult because you must surrender both the victim and villain mentality. As previously mentioned, we are conditioned from a very young age to "fit in" with our families, religious and educational institutions, and society as a whole, which often results in our reliance upon someone or something outside ourselves to give us the answers, direct us, or act on our behalf. This disempowering way of being gives away our "sense of power and responsibility" over our lives. It also sets the stage for mediocrity and resentment. Mediocrity is the standard of a victim. Resentment is long-standing anger directed toward the villains that supposedly keeps us in the role of victim. The truth is, we come from the Source that created all things. We have been given the ability and authority to "create" through our thoughts and feelings. Therefore, your beliefs (conscious or unconscious) become reality, and your feelings fuel the expediency or delay of your manifestation. Once you accept this Universal Law, you begin to realize that your power resides inside and that your thoughts and emotions are a choice. That means you and no one else is responsible for what happens in your life. The rule of thumb, as stated by Spiritual Life Coach Malane Shani, is, *"Everything in your life begins and ends with you."* The Law is not meant to shame or guilt you, but to get you to understand that when you own it, you can change it. If you wait on others to change, it may never happen, so stop blaming external forces. Whatever experience you encounter, know that you are consciously or unconsciously creating it in order to teach you something. You will repeat the lesson as many times as needed until you integrate and grow. This new way of viewing life will completely shift how you see your experiences, make decisions and interact with others. You will learn to value life's challenges and at the same time become very intentional about every action you take, or don't take. Self-responsibility is the power of choice.

Your Homework:

- ✓ In every situation, become present to your options and make intentional choices (i.e. I could do this or that, but I am choosing this).

- ✓ When you experience undesired consequences, remind yourself that you made the best possible decision in the moment *and* you can choose again in the present moment.

- ✓ Take others and their needs into consideration but make your decisions based on what is best for you. Take ownership of your life. Run your own race and live with the consequences and rewards.

3.   **M**anagement:

Self-management is the practice of repetition and routine. This requires you to become comfortable with change, discipline and accountability, for in doing so you will get to see who you are today, where you need more development, and how to supervise and deal with yourself. Contrary to what many people believe, change does not have to be difficult. It is the *resistance* to change that makes it painful. Let me explain. You have a Twin Nature – Spirit (intangible self) and Humanness (tangible self). Your Spirit welcomes change because it knows this is how we learn and grow. Your Humanness (which includes your physical body and brain) prefers consistency over change because (1) it wants to ensure your survival and what you have been doing thus far has worked – even if it has been destructive; and (2) it does not want you to experience any discomfort that may be associated with change. The physical body is designed to carry out the directives of your beliefs and feelings. Thus, the trick here is to watch and control your thoughts and feelings related to change, discipline and accountability.

When confronted with change, internal accountability is where you begin. Listen closely and you will see just how clever you are in convincing yourself that "you can't", "you shouldn't", or "something / someone else is a barrier or priority." This is where discipline must kick in. First, go back to the practices of Self-Acceptance (integrity/vulnerability) and Self-Responsibility (ownership). Tell yourself the truth and remind yourself that this is about you loving yourself enough to forge ahead. Take full responsibility for anything that you are creating in the way of obstacles. Next, discipline yourself by creating a regular routine that is realistic but stretches you beyond your comfort zone. This will eliminate all excuses. Make sure the routine has lots of repetition. Remember, all habits - empowering and disempowering - are formed through replication. The last and probably the most important component of Self-Management is internal and external accountability. Internally, you must hold yourself accountable. We do this in a kind but firm way. It is counterproductive to judge, shame, villainize or victimize ourselves, as this will only make us want to give up or resort to old ways of being. To hold yourself accountable, simply remind yourself of who you say you are and how important living this truth is for you to become the next version of self. Stand in integrity and call yourself out when you are giving your power away or making excuses. Next, get back on course. The tools in this book will also help you to see when and where you are strongest and the areas in which you need improvement.

External accountability is also critical to the process of change and, in my experience, is one of the most valuable and underutilized resources. This type of accountability entails sharing what you are doing and asking for constructive feedback from a trusted and supportive family member or friend; hiring a coach; or joining a community of likeminded people. If you are uncomfortable sharing, being vulnerable and you avoid external accountability systems, you should note, this is yet another clever and evasive tactic of your Humanness. This brings me to the final thought around Self-Management: good feedback is invaluable. Because you cannot totally see your own strengths or shortcomings, you need a 360-degree lens. However, depending on your personality, the timing, and who the feedback is coming from, you may take that feedback personally. This is when it is important to know yourself. If you know you tend to take things personally (like me), prepare yourself first. Remind yourself to be open and that you have created this feedback to show you something valuable. If you know that you are already down in the dumps, give yourself twenty-four hours before asking for feedback. During this time, allow yourself to be in your feelings but then take ownership of where you are and responsibility for getting yourself out of it and back on course. Finally, be very deliberate about selecting friends and family members as accountability partners. Not everyone is capable of lending constructive support. Some people will tell you, "You don't need to do this" and "You are being too hard on yourself," while others may be overly critical. Everyone is speaking from where they are in their development. You are looking for sincere, straightforward feedback. The rule of thumb is, "Take what resonates with your Spirit and leave the rest."

Your Homework:

    ✓ Establish at least three external accountability systems (i.e. a supportive but honest friend; a coach or therapist; a community of likeminded people).

    ✓ Establish regular routines with specific measures of success.

    ✓ Check in regularly on your progress and hold yourself accountable for what you say you are going to do. When you fall short, acknowledge it and get right back on course. As you make progress, acknowledge and affirm your wins.

Finally, a word to the wise. As stated earlier, mindset is everything and feelings ain't fact. Physiologically, our thoughts and feelings both come from our brain and, contrary to what you might think, they feed off each other. What you believe or think triggers a feeling and how you interpret that feeling will determine the corresponding action. Or, you can have a feeling and it will prompt a thought about what the feeling means. Thoughts and feelings are constantly changing depending upon one's experience and interpretation. The key is to not be attached to them, for just because you feel a certain way doesn't mean that is the truth. Also remember that there are no inherently good or bad feelings. While certain feelings (i.e. joyful, powerful and peaceful) are energizing, they are no more normal or acceptable than feelings of fear, sadness and anger. To be human and experience all of life's highs and lows, we need to access the full spectrum of feelings. The goal is to avoid getting stuck in a low or high feeling. Throughout your 40-Day Journey, commit to being open; let go of old beliefs and replace them with ones that support the life you desire; maintain a positive attitude and embrace the full range of feelings. To support you in managing your feelings, use the 6:24 rule below.

6:24 Rule

Step 1: Know your triggers.

Step 2: Look for indicators of fear, anger, denial, resistance, guilt, shame, et cetera.

Step 3: When you recognize a feeling, you have six seconds to decide if you can process through it immediately or if you need twenty-four hours.

Step 4: When you are ready, stay present and be aware of who is leading – Spirit or Humanness.

Step 5: Acknowledge the feeling by labeling it (i.e. *"I feel fearful, angry or guilty. I'm not ready to deal with this situation."*).

Step 6: Honor the feeling by suspending judgment or rejecting the truth (i.e. Refrain from saying, *"I feel this way but I shouldn't"* or *"I'm not angry"* when you truly are).

Step 7: Look for the lesson. Keep the focus on owning this experience as an opportunity for you to grow (i.e. *What is this trigger, event or person here to teach me? How can this benefit me?*)

Step 8: Demonstrate gratitude. Give thanks for yet another opportunity to see yourself.

Step 9: Decide to let go and heal all resentment (*mindfulness practices like meditation or visualization can aid you with this step*). Practice trusting and letting things flow.

Step 10: When you experience a major incident and you are having trouble regrouping, give yourself twenty-four hours to isolate, rant, pout, wallow or express your feelings in a way that doesn't bring harm to yourself and others. Ask for help from your external community when needed. Then go back to Steps 3-8.

Learn Through Experiences

The bulk of your journey to becoming a master of yourself will be *Learning Through Experiences*. In other words, this is not a one-and-done course. "It's You Against You: How to Master Life and Win at Being You" is designed to help you pinpoint and transform the habits that are keeping you from living your best life. The book provides two categories of experiences, *Principles of Self-Mastery* and *Principles of Self-Care*. You will learn to utilize both.

Principles of Self-Mastery

There are twenty Principles of Self-Mastery, which are designed to counteract the most pervasive self-sabotaging beliefs, attitudes and habits. <u>You will select only *one* principle to focus upon during a 40-day window.</u> Before making your selection, I recommend that you first read through the ***Ponder This*** section of each principle. You will likely have several that you could work on but there will be one that is calling for you to address *urgently*. You can use this course as many times as you'd like; you can repeat the same principle or select a new one. The choice is yours. Remember, this is lifelong work. There is no need to hurry through all the principles because, as Malane Shani says, "Practice makes permanent – not perfect."

Each Self-Mastery Principle has ten components. The first five components focus on discovery and will be completed on Day 1 of the Journey. Please note, you will need a journal (of sorts) throughout the process.

DAY 1: DISCOVERY

1. **Self-Love Principle and Number**

2. **Pre and Post Assessment:** A sample of the Pre/Post Assessments can be found on Pg. 79 in the Tools section. You may copy the tool or replicate the content in a journal.

3. **Ponder This**: This is a thought-provoking phrase that introduces you to the concept and sets the stage for working with it.

4. **Faith Your Fear**: This section thoroughly explains the principle, the problems it creates when it is out of balance, and a proposed solution.

5. **Be Inspired**: This enables you to connect with and be inspired through a heartfelt and insightful testimonial from an individual who is experienced in the principle.

Then, over Days 2 through 40, you will gradually work on Components 6-10. This part of the principle is designed to help you practice, learn and reflect on your experiences.

DAYS 2-40: PRACTICE & REFLECTION

6. **Coach's Corner**: As an optional support, you can visit the "Coach's Corner" on the website. Here, Coach Tracey shares the common stumbling blocks associated with the principle and quick tips to avoid the pitfalls and optimize success.

7. **Practice Self-Mastery**: This section offers you a choice of recommended routines, exercises, or actions that will enable you to foster a new or more consistent pattern through daily or weekly practice. Additional activities may also be found on the website at www.iamtraceyknight.com

8. **Daily Affirmations**: This section offers you a choice of three mantras to affirm throughout your day to aid you in reprogramming old and disempowering beliefs.

9. **Plan & Track Your Progress**: A sample Plan and Track Your Progress tool can be found in the Tool section on page 79. You have the choice of photocopying the template in this book or recreating the content in a journal.

10. **Self-Care**: You will be asked to select one to three Principles of Self-Care to support you during the 40-Day experience. Select from any of the 20 options listed on pages 68-77.

A proposed schedule has been created for you in a subsequent section entitled *Scheduling and Maximizing Your 40-Day Journey*.

Principles of Self-Care

WHAT IS SELF-CARE? Do you know the difference between self-care and selfishness? Putting ourselves first can trigger feelings of guilt and shame, especially if it is in lieu of doing for the people who mean the most to us. Oftentimes we give until we are mentally, emotionally, physically and even financially depleted. Why? Is it to please and earn the love of another?

Self-care is about *unapologetically* prioritizing ourselves and our needs. This is not selfish. It's an act of self-love. What do you need? What do you want? What would make you happy? How can you express devotion towards yourself? You can begin by incorporating one to three of the 20 Principles of Self-Care listed in the back of the book into your 40-Day Journey. They have been designed to cultivate a stronger and more loving connection with the person you spend the most time with - you. You can also come up with your own practices, so long as you are consistent in your implementation.

Scheduling and Maximizing Your 40-Day Journey

The 40-Day Journey will require an average of 15 to 20 minutes per day. I suggest allocating 30 minutes at the start of each week to re-read the principle, reflect on the prior week's experiences and devise a plan for the week ahead. Since some principles result in a work product (i.e. creating a vision board or growing a plant), you may want to allocate time each week to gradually work on completing it by the end of the journey. Other *Principles of Self-Mastery* simply require you to be aware and managed in your daily interactions. In either case, an average of 15 minutes should be earmarked each evening to track your efforts, progress and state of being in the tool listed on pages 68-77. Since you control your schedule and how you implement the activities, there should be few time constraints and excuses, thereby increasing your internal accountability.

Day 0

» Familiarize yourself with each *Principle of Self Mastery* by reviewing the *Ponder This* section.

» <u>Select one *Principle of Self-Mastery* to focus upon for the 40-Day Journey</u>. This should be the one that resonates with you the most.

» Review the *Ponder This* section of each of the *Principles of Self-Care*. Select at least one but no more than three Principles of Self-Care to focus on for the duration of the journey. Again, the goal is to become proficient through consistent practice, rather than giving yourself a lot of busywork to do.

» Take the **40-Day Pre Assessments** to help you examine how consistently you practice the selected *Principle of Self-Mastery* and *Principle of Self-Care*. This will create a baseline for assessing growth. The same process will be repeated at the end of the process on Day 41 (found in the Tool section beginning on page 77).

» Begin gathering any supplies that are called for in the **Practice Self-Mastery** section (found in the Tool section beginning on page 77). Regardless of your selected principle, it will be helpful to have a journal that you can use during the 40-Day Journey.

» Complete the following Pre-Journey Ritual, "Dear Me!"

   o When was the last time you received a love letter? Why wait on someone else to do what you can do for yourself?

   o Instructions: Gather a separate sheet of paper(s) and an envelope. Take 15 minutes to write a passionate love letter to you. Open with the salutation "Dear Me," then talk about why you are taking the 40-Day Journey. Why do you want to become a master of your life in this area? What do you intend to accomplish and how do you believe it will help you? Discuss what you value and appreciate most about yourself; perhaps it is your courage, faith or vision for your life. End the letter with "I LOVE YOU!" Sign your name and seal it in the envelope. Put it in a place where you will remember to access it at the end of the journey.

   o Check out an example of "Dear Me" love letter on my website, www.IAMTRACEYKNIGHT.com

Day 1

» Read your selected *Principles of Self Mastery* in totality (*the Self-Mastery Principle, Number, Ponder This, Faith Your Fear, and Conversation of the Heart*).

» Write a reflection on how the **Faith Your Fear** narrative relates to your life and experiences. If you need more space than provided, insert sheets or use your journal.

Days 2-40

» At the start of each week, re-read the **Practice Self Mastery.** Create a weekly plan to incorporate this recommended routine or exercise(s).

» Reflect on the **Coach's Corner**. Remain aware of how the stumbling block(s) may crop up. Use the quick tips to avoid the pitfalls and optimize success.

» Select one of the three affirmations. Affirm it throughout the day to aid in reprogramming old and disempowering beliefs.

» Each day/week, **Track, Reflect and Rate Your Progress** using the tool found on pages 68-76

» As often as possible, incorporate one to three **Principles of Self-Care** to support you during the 40-Day experience.

Day 41

» Take the **40-Day Post Assessments** found in the Tool section beginning on page 77 to evaluate how consistently you are now practicing the targeted *Principle of Self-Mastery* and *Principle(s) of Self-Care*. Compare your two Likert Scale ratings and *celebrate* your growth – expediential, incremental or nominal. All growth is great!

» Post-Journey Ritual, "Dear Me!"

  o Open the love letter you wrote to yourself at the start of the 40-Day Journey.

  o Reflect:

    ▪ How does it feel to see how much you are appreciated, adored and admired by yourself for accepting this challenge?

    ▪ What advice or support would you give the person who wrote the letter 40 days earlier?

  o Give yourself a hug. Affirm your hard work and, again, don't forget to celebrate!

PRINCIPLES OF SELF-MASTERY

Self-Mastery Principle # 1
Honor Your Truth

 PONDER THIS

Who are you?

 **FAITH YOUR FEAR**

Personal integrity is the cornerstone of self-love. Integrity is more than behaving ethically and above reproach with others. It is telling yourself the truth, regardless of the outcome (Honesty); being able to depend on yourself to follow through with what you say you will do for yourself (Trustworthiness); and living a life that is guided by a set of standards that you set for yourself (Character).

When we are unclear about or out of alignment with our own values, beliefs, feelings, opinions and actions, it is nearly impossible for us to keep our word, commitments and promises to ourselves, let alone others. We begin to solidify our relationship with ourselves by fortifying our foundation and then maintaining a steadfast commitment to honoring our truth – even if it is not popular with others. The quiet voice inside (Spirit) knows the truth of "who we are" and uses our intuition to signal us when we behave out of character. We can also reconnect with and use our values as a guidepost for all decisions and interactions.

 **BE INSPIRED**
Christina Cruz Benton

"To thine own self, be true." – William Shakespeare

Most of us know this quote, yet we stumble upon the meaning of truth.

For me, it's honesty, integrity, good health, trustworthiness and peace. I'd like to think that I've always possessed those qualities; I also hoped that my personal relationships embodied those same qualities of truth.

But what happens when you abandon your ability to be your own "truth-teller"? After years of not facing my truth, the chickens came home to roost. My life as the perfect wife and mother imploded/exploded and my confused expectations of myself as a people-pleaser, responsible for others, suddenly came into focus. I began delving into the truth about my life, my upbringing, and my relationships. The truth was that I had spent thirty-nine years with a man who lied to me day in, day out. There were many signs, many clues, many inner-whispers that told me the truth, but I had chosen to ignore them.

It's taken me almost a lifetime to understand that Shakespeare's words represent the paramount act of self-love.

I would like to say that I see it all so clearly now, but the truth is that the lens is still a bit foggy. That's okay, though, because I am a work in progress. With the loving assistance of those I call my "truth-tellers," I am slowly piecing my life together. I do feel that for the first time I am on solid ground, taking it easy and, with the help of my Higher Power, taking it one day at a time. Today, I demand honesty, integrity, good health, trustworthiness, and above all – peace.

"To thine own self, I can and will be true."

 PRACTICE SELF-MASTERY

Activity #1

Make a list of your top 25 values. Next, pare down the list to five (5) core values and clarify what each value means to you. Memorize the list.

Activity #2

To create standards, explore how you will apply these values in each area of your life (i.e. career, finances, love/intimacy, family, spirituality, having fun, and health/fitness). Write a set of standards that will serve as a guideline for how you will operate.

Example: The value is Open Communication. The standard is "I actively listen and honestly communicate my feelings and position in a way that is honoring of me and respectful of others."

Activity #3

Now ask and answer these questions:
"What do I need to do to embody my values and standards? How will I hold myself accountable?"

Practice: Look for times in your daily interactions when you are challenged or less likely to uphold your values, especially when it's not personally rewarding or may be displeasing to others.

Remember, you live a life of integrity because of who you say you are, not to impress or appease others.

AFFIRM YOUR INTENTION

- I trust myself.
- I value (insert your 5 core values).
- I honor my truth.

PRACTICE SELF-CARE

- Select a self-love activity from the back of the book to practice for 40 days.

Self-Mastery Principle # 2
Intentionally Create the Life You Desire!

 PONDER THIS

What would you envision for yourself if you knew you would succeed, be loved, be approved of, and had all the time and resources you needed?

 FAITH YOUR FEAR

We often put limits on the vision we have for our life because we are afraid of failing, disappointing ourselves, or that the outcome will be different than we expect. These beliefs limit our imagination and the opportunity to grow into our full potential. The only limits are the ones we place upon ourselves. We can be assured that "Where there is vision, there is also provision."

- Unknown

 **BE INSPIRED**
Cyndi Burton

At the base of Self-love is intentionality. In order to fulfill desire, you must be intentional. Whether the goal is to obtain a certain weight, or in my case, find a job that would launch my career, the first step is focusing on the desire. Before starting this journey towards Self-Mastery, I was afraid to embrace my inner desires or set my intention toward them, because it required me to be vulnerable. It required me to stand up to my inner doubts. "Am I qualified enough?", "How will I ever find a job right out of college that allows me to be flexible?", "Maybe I should just take this job 'for now.'" If it was not for learning how to be intentional, I would have created a life of settling. A life of "maybe next year." Through intentionality I was able to stay focused on my desires and begin living the life I always saw for myself.

15

 **PRACTICE SELF-MASTERY**

Activity #1

First, sit quietly and visualize your best life. Where would you go? What would you accomplish? Allow yourself to feel what it feels like to have the life you desire. Set 10 minutes aside each day to repeat this process through meditation. Use your five senses to immerse yourself in the experience of living your ideal life.

Activity #2

Next, write about it in your journal. What would you be doing? You can repeat this process as often as you like. Post it where you can review it each day.

Activity #3

Finally, identify at least one step you can take to bring you closer to your vision. Take immediate action, no matter how small. When that action is complete, repeat the process.

Activity #4

Focus on taking consistent and actionable steps, not how long it will take to get to the finish line. Remember, It's the journey to the "peak of the pyramid" that matters the most.

 AFFIRM YOUR INTENTION

• The life I desire is in my sight.

• Every time I fail, I learn a new way to succeed.

• Onward! Everything I need is being provided.

 PRACTICE SELF-CARE

• Select a self-love activity from the back of the book to practice for 40 days

Self-Mastery Principle # 3
Live Authentically.

 PONDER THIS

How often do you change, shrink, modify, ignore or silence yourself to please others?

Are you courageous enough to be unapologetically you?

 FAITH YOUR FEAR

We have been socialized to believe that who we are is not good enough. Thus, we spend most of our time and energy defining ourselves, selecting goals, making decisions and choosing relationships based on the following beliefs:

"I am what I look like.";

"I am what I have.";

"I am what I do.";

"I am what achieve.";

"I am what others think about me.";

"I must compare myself and compete with others.";

"I am on my own in this life."

We look at our physical appearance and criticize it as too short/tall, fat/thin/curvy/stout, or some other perceived deficiency. We may believe that we aren't smart enough, can't manage money, or that our personality is too strong or weak, silly or weird. We may feel that we need a mate, degree or title in order to be acceptable.

These beliefs keep us from being authentic. The deep desire to "fit in" and please others slowly diminishes the awareness of our truth as well as the courage to pursue it without guilt or shame.

When we seek others' approval or validation over our own, we become a slave to self-loathing, belittlement, shyness, sloth and perfectionism. We can only be our "best self" when we know we are acceptable just as we are right now. Remember, if your Higher Power made it, it's good enough.

Are we really willing to sacrifice our own happiness, health and peace of mind just to get approval or to make someone else feel good about us?

 **BE INSPIRED**
Angela Jackson

While in college I worked the front desk of a large hotel. I had my nose pierced over Thanksgiving break. My manager, who was Caucasian, asked me to remove my nose ring while at work. When I pointed out that

17

the women in housekeeping had nose rings, he replied, "They are Indian and that is their culture." I looked him in his face and said, "My family and culture is African, so don't talk to me about heritage." It was in that moment that I stood up for who I am and what I felt was an authentic representation of myself. Thirty-two years later, I am successfully working in corporate America with my nose ring in.

 **PRACTICE SELF-MASTERY**

Activity #1

Reprogram your beliefs about yourself. With Joe Cocker's "You Are So Beautiful" playing in the background, stand in the mirror and look at your nude body. Focus on the areas that you believe to be less appealing; then single out parts of your body and state why you appreciate each one. For example, "Nose, you are so beautiful and I am grateful that you allow me to smell"; or "Throat, you are so beautiful and I am grateful to have a voice that speaks my truth."

Now conduct the same exercise as you look for other attributes, qualities, skills, or quirks that make you unique. Repeat this exercise daily.

In your journal, describe why/how they benefit your life.

How do they make you stronger, powerful, resilient, etc.?

Do this exercise as you listen to Whitney Houston's "I Didn't Know My Own Strength."

Repeat this exercise at least once a week.

Activity #2

Create your own affirmations to support this new belief. Select three statements (i.e. "I am brilliant"; "I am sexy"; "I am loveable."), then, using a voice recorder on your mobile phone, record yourself stating each one 7 times. As you get into bed each night, turn the recording on a low but audible volume; listen to them as you fall asleep (if you don't fall asleep during the first "cycle" replay the recording). This will begin to reprogram your subconscious mind. Note how you feel week after week.

Activity #3

Throughout your day, look for times when you are inclined to shrink, modify, seek approval, ignore your instincts or silence yourself because of an old belief about yourself. Catch it and check in by asking, "What do I authentically believe, want or need?" Give yourself permission to speak and honor your truth.

 AFFIRM YOUR INTENTION

• My approval is the only approval I need.

PRACTICE SELF-CARE

• Select a self-love activity from the back of the book to practice for 40 days

Self-Mastery Principle # 4
It's You Against You.

 PONDER THIS

The greatest asset and challenge you have is staring at you in the mirror.

You will never become who you are capable of being if you only play to your strengths and ignore your weaknesses and wounds.

 **FAITH YOUR FEAR**

You have two choices, stay where you are (which is likely a mediocre version of your true self) or grow and become the full version of who you are intended to be. Most people want more for their life (i.e. more health, meaning, love, prosperity, success, joy, etc.) but they either do not know how or are unwilling to do what it takes to get it.

The "how" refers to the willingness to uncover, confront and conquer hidden, internal obstacles. These barriers are typically rooted in fear or feelings of inadequacy or unworthiness. They are unconsciously masked in excuses, reasoning, indifference or disinterest to keep us from facing a few simple truths:

(1) We are the only thing standing in the way of our greatness; (2) We have the power to make a change but it's going to require serious and consistent effort; and (3) The process is not going to be easy and we will likely have to work through painful experiences.

You are exactly who the fears in your mind say you are until you confront them.

The "what it takes" is the unrelenting commitment to seek out and take on your fears, weaknesses and emotional wounds until their power over your life is diminished or eliminated. If you think you can't run, you must become a runner. If you are afraid of public speaking, you must take on speaking engagements. If you are afraid of failing, you must put yourself in environments where you will fail and learn – fail and learn. If you are afraid of being hurt or judged in relationships, you must become more open and vulnerable. We are socialized to play to our strengths and downplay our weaknesses. Our strengths are valuable tools and confirmation that we are capable of mastery. However, it is our weaknesses and emotional wounds that diminish our power and keep us stuck. The mind is what you create. As you conquer your fears and overcome the barriers of the mind, opportunities become endless. To know your greatness, you must intentionally and regularly put yourself in experiences that will show you "who you are" and what you are capable of becoming.

Decide! Face you or be defeated by you.

BE INSPIRED
Tracey Knight

I realize that I have allowed fear to rule most of my life. Most of my decisions have been deliberate and cautious because I wanted to avoid the humiliation of failure; I was afraid of not being good enough; or I felt I did not deserve and/or could not handle something more. Though these beliefs existed in every area of my life, it has been most apparent in my physical body. Growing up, I thought and affirmed to myself, "I can't run short or long distances. My heart beats too fast and I could hurt myself." Consequently, every time I had to run, I felt anxiety, resistance and my heart would race to the point where I would stop. I've grown to understand that my words have power and they come from my beliefs. Whatever I believe and say enough times becomes true for me. In 2018, I decided I wanted to run. I already had a rigorous cardio workout and logically, there was really no reason why my heart could not withstand the intensity of running. On my first effort, I ran a sprint, but my chest felt like it would explode. My breathing was off. A runner friend of mine suggested that I slow down the pace to teach myself how to breathe. At a steady but slower pace, I began running and was able to complete a one-mile run. I kept practicing, adding more distance rather than speed. Now, after a year, I am running at a moderate pace for longer stints of time. I realized that it was the fear of the unknown and repetitive pessimistic thoughts that were standing in my way. Once I made the decision that running was what I was going to do, I shifted my thinking and committed to a practice. With small incremental progress, I can now say, "I am a runner!"

PRACTICE SELF-MASTERY

Make a list of your shortcomings, failures, fears and things that make you feel inadequate or uncertain. You can include small things like "I can only do one pushup" or "I am afraid of snakes," as well as more significant undertakings such as "I am afraid to start a business, finish my book or climb Mount Everest." Categorize them as such. This list will evolve over time, so don't get caught up in how many items are initially included.

Next, select a one small and one significant quest to conquer. Every single day…every opportunity you get… put yourself in the environment to start facing and chipping away at this barrier. Get in the habit of taking some sort of action every day / week, depending on the undertaking. Keep your charge at the forefront of your mind by doing visualizations or create a small vision board exclusively for this quest. Document your efforts in your journal.

Instead of saying, "I can't do this or that" make yourself good enough through relentless, repetitive practice.

Instead of avoiding difficult situations, lean into the experiences that are most challenging. Look at how you react, what you say to yourself and how you feel. Look for times when you offer up excuses, rationalizations, indifference and disinterest. This is your kryptonite and a recipe for mediocrity. Keep going and rep it out through practice.

Instead of settling for less than what you want or deserve, go after the impossible and make it possible.

The process includes:

*Becoming obsessed and driven about becoming a better version of "you."

*Embracing failure as a resource for feeding you information about how you handle weakness and the areas in which you need more development.

*Tell yourself the truth. Don't lie or deceive yourself. If you are overweight, acknowledge it, not to berate or punish yourself, but as a matter of factual information that is unacceptable to you. Then take action.

*Make it a practice to always do a little more and a little more…and a little more in every situation. If you have to do 10 situps, do 11, 12 or 13. Go the extra mile.

 ## AFFIRM YOUR INTENTION

- Every time I face a fear, weakness or wound, I get stronger.

- I am inventing a better version of me.

- I am comfortable with being uncomfortable. I can handle anything that comes my way (i.e. failure, judgement, ridicule, suffering, pain).

 ## PRACTICE SELF-CARE

- Select a self-love activity from the back of the book to practice for 40 days

Self-Mastery Principle # 5
Become Your Own B.F.F.

 PONDER THIS

Are you your friend or your enemy?

 FAITH YOUR FEAR

A friend creates a trusting environment where you feel safe. Friends are loyal, empathetic and non-judgmental. Friends are honest and lend support as they hold you accountable for becoming your best self. Conversely, an enemy is someone who actively opposes you and your efforts to be "great." Their behavior (overt or covert) can be distracting, deviating, deceiving and adversarial and it can cause real harm. You can determine whether you are your ally or your foe by examining what you believe to be true about yourself. Are you judgmental or affirming in your communication to and about yourself? Do your actions say that you can depend on you to follow through on what you say you are going to do?"

Your confidence and ability to accomplish the smallest and largest goals is directly correlated to your relationship with yourself. You create your life. As Mahatma Gandhi once said, "Your thoughts create words. Your words create action. Your actions create habits. Your habits create character and your character creates your destiny." Begin to reframe how you relate to yourself. Be your friend, not your foe.

 **BE INSPIRED**
Nikki Turner

I come from a long line of "outside" believers — that is, I was reared to believe that happiness comes from outside myself. Outside people made me feel loved, outside material possessions made me feel happy/rich, and outside recognition made me feel worthy. It should come as no surprise, then, that I believed that a "BFF" was also someone outside of oneself. Today, after reading, receiving, and following the path of self-examination and self-reflection found in Tracey Knight's dynamic treatise of self-love, "It's You Against You: 40 Principles to Help You Master Life and Win at Being You," this is no longer the case. I now understand that a BFF should start with oneself!! A BFF is someone with whom you can be completely transparent and laugh abundantly. Your BFF also knows all your secrets but never judges or shuns, a person who tells you both what you want to hear AND that which you need to hear. There is truly no greater or more ideal love than the love of a BFF. Thank you, Tracey!! Forty days later, I now know that I am complete! I am love! I am on purpose! I AM my own BFF!!

🏃 PRACTICE SELF-MASTERY

Since your confidence and ability to accomplish the smallest and largest goals is directly correlated to your relationship with yourself, let's use one of your goals as a platform for examining and correcting disempowering habits.

First, identify a friendship / relationship that you admire because of the support the individuals lend to one another. If you don't have a living example, use a movie or create a fictious one. List the magnificent qualities of the relationship, including how they interact when there is conflict or someone needs to have a difficult conversation or be held accountable. You will adopt their characteristics as a part of your friendship profile with yourself.

Now select a personal, professional, financial or health goal that you want to achieve but have yet to accomplish.

Next, examine your beliefs.

What do you think about yourself and your ability to achieve success in this area? Why haven't you accomplished the goal thus far? Remember to keep the focus on you and not distractions created by others. Take full ownership of why you have not achieved the success you desire.

Where did the belief come from? Recall the characteristics of a good friend and ask yourself, how would such a friend support you through disempowering beliefs? What would they think about your potential? How would they lend support? What new and more empowering beliefs might they offer to replace the old beliefs?

Next, examine your language. How do you speak about this goal and your ability to achieve it? How would your friend speak to you about this goal? How would they encourage and hold you accountable? Reframe your language to encourage strength and resiliency.

Finally, examine your behaviors and habits. Where are you engaging in self-sabotaging actions? What did you fail to do because you were afraid? Are you blaming or using others as an excuse? How have your habitual practices led to you settling for less than what you desired? How would your friend support and hold you accountable in a loving way?

To strengthen your confidence and better support yourself, identify at least one proactive measure you can take today to move toward your desired outcome. Continue practicing and holding yourself to account. Where you fall short, do not spend time chastising, just make amends to yourself and continue working toward alignment.

ACTIVITY 2

Practice taking yourself on friend dates, either in or out of the house. Carve out time weekly to spend quality time with your BFF.

ACTIVITY 3

Go to the mirror each day and talk to your BFF. Affirm him/her. Hold them accountable. Acknowledge their presence, beauty and lend support when needed.

AFFIRM YOUR INTENTION

- I am my own best friend.
- I have the power to change.
- What I believe becomes true for me. Thus, I choose only empowering thoughts, words and actions.

♥ **PRACTICE SELF-CARE**

- Select a self-love activity from the back of the book to practice for 40 days

Self-Mastery Principle # 6
You Are Most Powerful When You Harmonize Your Masculine and Feminine Energy.

 ## PONDER THIS

Did you know you can optimize your self-confidence and ability to relate to others by knowing how and when to leverage the power of your masculine and feminine qualities?

 ## FAITH YOUR FEAR

The world is comprised of polar opposites that work together to create harmony (i.e. up/down, light/dark, still/active, gentle power/forceful power, creative/analytical). Such is true for human beings. We have a Twin Nature - Humanness (masculine) and Spirit (feminine). These aspects of our person have nothing to do with gender or sexuality. Masculine energy can be intellectual, convincing, fixed, giving and action-oriented. In its extreme, it is also controlling, competitive, domineering, and individualized. Feminine energy is receptive, intuitive, creative, flexible, allowing and inclusive. In its extreme, it is overly emotional, indecisive, unproductive, and conforming. We are socialized to believe that to be dominant is strength and to feel is to be weak. However, the ability to feel, be instinctively guided and to connect with others are critical traits, especially when making decisions and relating or working with others. When we deny or minimize the importance of any aspect of our self, we diminish our value and throw life off balance. Can plants grow without water? No, but too much water will wash away the seedlings and soil. There is a time and space for everything – our individual accomplishments and working in community; giving and receiving; leading and following; boldness and mellowness. When we use both our thinking and feeling natures to assess a situation and guide our actions, we have a greater chance to respond in a way that is healthy for us and respectful of others.

 ## BE INSPIRED
Shaka Singleton

As a man raised in a masculine-dominated society I personally lean tremendously on my intelligence, ability to detach emotionally, and exterior strength as a means to navigate and engage in my relationships. These qualities are awesome to have; however, I've learned to open myself up to my feminine side which is more loving, authentic, supportive, and allowing of myself and others. This has proven extremely powerful in my relationships with women, particularly in my current relationship. I am able to share my true emotions, be vulnerable with my heart, and trust her to be who she is and myself to be who I am. I've tapped into unconditional love at a deeper level and it's taken my experience in life to another level because I trust myself and what I'm creating even more.

25

PRACTICE SELF-MASTERY

Activity 1:

Name your Twin Nature so that you will be able to recognize the differences in their voices, personalities and behavioral extremes.

As you move through your day, try to differentiate between your two natures. Ask yourself, who/what qualities are needed in this moment and then take action accordingly. Observe what happens when one nature is used at an inappropriate time (i.e. you used force when gentleness was needed).

Activity 2:

While in the midst of a highly emotional experience practice labeling your feelings (i.e. happy, sad, scared, joyful, powerful, mad or peaceful) and expressing them to someone you trust. Feel the power of owning your true feelings.

Activity 3:

Consider taking the first unit in the Master Your Life Course to help you better understand how to manage and integrate your Spirit and Humanness.

AFFIRM YOUR INTENTION

- I am self-aware and self-managed.
- I am most powerful when I honor the wholeness of me.
- I am intuitively guided but strategically aimed.

PRACTICE SELF-CARE

- Select a self-love activity from the back of the book to practice for 40 days.

Self-Mastery Principle # 7
Embrace Failure.

 PONDER THIS

"Failure isn't fatal and failure isn't forever." -Bill Pickard

To succeed in life, you must fail fast and frequently.

 FAITH YOUR FEAR

In sciences classes, students learn that failure is a welcomed and essential part of the scientific process. However, in school, and in life, we are often penalized for making mistakes. In truth, failure is a valuable mechanism for learning. As we experiment with various ways of tackling an issue, we grow from discovering what works and what does not. The real reason we despise failure is the fear of appearing weak and/or disappointing others. When we avoid or measure our worth by failure, we chase external approval while ruining opportunities to grow. The more we fail, the stronger we become.

 **BE INSPIRED**
Dasia Newman

During my senior year at Spelman College, I applied to be one of the Top 50 Women of Excellence at the same time I was preparing to apply for a Fellowship at Harvard University and a full-time position with an investment firm in New York City. As you can imagine, these opportunities were highly competitive. There was a time when I felt as though I was not good enough to even apply but I mustered up the courage to pursue goals that seemed outlandish for someone like me. Shortly after submitting my application to the selection committee of the Women of Excellence and Leadership Program, I received a denial letter. This confirmed the belief that I was unworthy. I began to convince myself that I did not need to apply for the Harvard Fellowship or the high-powered job in New York because I would just be setting myself up for failure. Thank goodness I was a part of a supportive community lead by Coach Tracey Knight. I felt inadequate and defeated but I knew I needed an objective ear. During my session with Tracey, she helped me see this denial letter through a different lens. I discovered that I attached my self-worth to my accomplishments. I was letting the denial letter define me and what I was able to achieve. I was prepared to give up everything because of one letter. After many tears and a big hug, Coach Tracey assured me that the best was yet to come. As soon as I let go of the labels people put on me, the expectations I put on myself, the competitive spirit I feel from other high-achievers, and the pressure to be "successful," I would see the true manifestation of what Spirit had in store for me. And I did. I let go of everything weighing me down and the next week, I received a correction email stating I *had* been admitted into the 2018 Class of Women of Excellence Scholars. A few weeks later, I was accepted into the Harvard Fellowship and I got the job in New York. Today, I recognize that failure, setbacks and disappoints are inevitable, and that the only real failure lies in not finding the lesson in the experience and being willing to try again.

 **PRACTICE SELF-MASTERY**

ACTIVITY 1:

Select an experience or goal at which you have previously failed or anticipate failing. Write out 6 scenarios (one for each week of the 40-Day Journey) that depicts how you could fail. Describe the potential lessons that could be learned and how you could grow from the experience. Next, brainstorm (in detail) the different ways you could handle the failure or obstacles. Talk about what you will do, what resources you will need and where you will get them. How long will it take you course correct? Acknowledge the areas where you are strong but recognize the places you need to improve. Pinpoint your mistakes and isolate the cause. Research best practices but don't be afraid to do it differently. Invest time testing, gathering data, learning and testing again. Explore how you can build a community of trusted confidants who will provide constructive feedback but will hold you accountable. Finally, check your thoughts. Make sure your beliefs, words and actions are in alignment with the success you seek. Explore how you will feel when you fail. How will you shift from dense to light feelings?

The purpose of this exercise is to help you to anticipate challenges, prepare and manage risks as you become comfortable with failure.

ACTIVTY 2:

Ask for constructive feedback. Don't take it as criticism; rather, give sincere thanks. Take what works, apply it and leave the rest.

ACTIVTY 3:

Seek out and put yourself in situations that feel unfamiliar, challenging, or where the outcome is unknown. Commit to completing one per week.

Possible examples include:

Drive a different way to work in the middle of rush hour. Eat an entire meal with your less dominant hand. Approach someone who is intimidating and give them a compliment. Challenge someone to a competitive activity or game you are unfamiliar with or not good at. Try a new restaurant or dish. Ask for a raise. Instinctively navigate your way to a destination without your GPS. Go to a dealership and drive the luxury car of your dreams. Make up and cook a new dish using the ingredients you already have in your house. Ask someone out on a date. Ride a bucking bull. Do an improve performance. Leave your phone off and at home for a full 24 hours. Take a stranger to lunch and have a conversation.

 AFFIRM YOUR INTENTION

- "Failure isn't fatal and failure isn't forever."
- I am willing to learn.
- Experience is the best teacher.

 PRACTICE SELF-CARE

- Select a self-love activity from the back of the book to practice for 40 days.

Self-Mastery Principle # 8
Plan Away Procrastination

 PONDER THIS

Often misinterpreted as laziness, the real culprit behind procrastination is fear of failure or success, or the perpetual need to be perfect.

But what comes first, procrastination or anxiety?

 FAITH YOUR FEAR

We avoid tasks hoping that something will change or go away. Instead, we create unnecessary anxiety that is further exacerbated by the embarrassment of having our inadequacies exposed; or even worst, succeeding and being burdened with increased expectations or responsibilities. This vicious vortex of doubt, worry, stress, guilt and shame creates a self-fulfilling prophecy that diminishes our self-esteem, affects our relationships and harms the body. We must challenge the distorted thinking that drives the behavior to waste time. Get into action! When we can use commitment and consistent effort to make small but practical changes in how we manage assignments, we will pluck out procrastination and anxiety at the root.

 **BE INSPIRED**
   Lisa McGee

Procrastination has been a barrier to my movement within the flow of life. I have come to embrace this as a reflection of my former fears of rejection, inadequacy, mediocrity and just simply falling short. I also recognize it as a nudge to get up and move and do - to make things happen. Procrastination is still there, but I now look at it as less of a barrier and more of a needed "kick ass" force that propels me into action.

PRACTICE SELF-MASTERY

Identify a place in your life where you are procrastinating and practice these steps:

First, be solution-oriented. We waste time constantly restating the problem and reprimanding ourselves for what we did or did not do. Instead, give yourself regular pep talks and promise yourself a healthy reward at the conclusion. Next, identify a couple of strategies that work best for you or the situation. For example, break tasks down into small chunks and schedule them out until the project is complete.

Tackle the hardest tasks first to get them out of the way.

Allocate a window of time to work on the project and set an alarm to mind the time.

Aim for progress not perfection and acknowledge the small wins. Use checkmarks or drawing a line through listed tasks to signal completion.

 AFFIRM YOUR INTENTION

- I am calm, centered and confident in my ability to handle whatever is put before me.
- I am betting on me. I won't let me down.

PRACTICE SELF-CARE

- Select a self-love activity from the back of the book to practice for 40 days.

Self-Mastery Principle # 9
Progress Not Perfection.

 PONDER THIS

Did you know that perfectionism is a form of self-abuse?

 **FAITH YOUR FEAR**

Perfectionism comes from fear. For some of us, it is fear of failure. If we fail, we will reveal to the world what we secretly believe about ourselves, that we are inadequate. This level of disappointment can't be stomached. So, we set an unachievable standard of being perfect. We try super hard, worrying, doubting and chastising our missteps along the way, and when we do complete the tasks, we focus on what went wrong instead of what went well. If we fell short of the intended outcome, we ridicule and convince ourselves that we just need to "do better."

Success is individualized and should be measured on a continuum of progress - not comparison to others. The goal is to compete with yourself to be better than you were yesterday and the day before that.

 **BE INSPIRED**
Valli Sears Jones

Progress <u>NOT</u> Perfection; <u>PROGRESS</u> not Perfection!

Prior to tackling this self-mastery principle, I always felt stressed about where I was headed in life. I had goals I wanted to reach, yet I hadn't fully formulated them in my mind. I could see the big picture, but sometimes the big picture was so big I didn't know what steps to take to get there. Sometimes, the worry about not being perfect prevented me from even starting to work toward my goal. It was as if I was stuck on a carousel, going around and around with no end in sight. I began repeating this loving affirmation – "Progress, not perfection!" out loud each day, until one morning I woke up and asked myself:

What's my "why"? What motivates me? What's my passion? My happiness? My definition of success? What outcome was I looking for? Am I doing God's work?

I was learning to focus on the journey, not the destination. Perfection, I realized, should never be the goal because the outcome will always be failure. Instead I strive for growth, improvement and learning while leaving wiggle room for imperfection. To ultimately be successful, I focus on the baby steps, small changes, and one-at-a-time steps along the path that will help me reach the bigger goals and a better me.

🏃 PRACTICE SELF-MASTERY

Select a project or task that you are attempting to make "perfect."

Define what success is for you.

What is motivating you?

Is this your passion?

Does it make you happy?

What outcome are you looking for and why?

Are you doing Spirit's work?

If you are satisfied with your answers and want to proceed, map out the path to your goal.

Break your task(s) up into bite-size chunks by identifying what must be done immediately and what would be nice to accomplish.

It is okay to make it S.M.A.R.T. (specific, measurable, attainable, realistic, and time-sensitive), but be careful. Rigidity can lead you right back into perfectionism. Refrain from being overzealous. The goal is to manage your expectations of yourself.

Now that you have a plan, accept that this will be an incremental process. Take action daily / weekly. As you move through the process, watch and track how things progress.

When there are glitches or things fall short of your desired outcome, recognize that that is also a part of the process. It is a learning opportunity. What is it teaching you? Refrain from chastising yourself or the process.

Note your incremental successes and accomplishments, rather than feeling like a failure because everything did not come together exactly how you envisioned it or because it looks different from the way others accomplished it.

In each moment, do your best and remember that your best can change based upon circumstances. Doing your best in the present moment is good enough.

AFFIRM YOUR INTENTION

- I always do my best.
- Progress, not perfection.
- Every day, I get better and better.

PRACTICE SELF-CARE

- Select a self-love activity from the back of the book to practice for 40 days.

Self-Mastery Principle # 10
It's Better to Give & Receive.

 ## PONDER THIS

Generosity and Reciprocity is one of the Universal Laws that not only governs our existence but tests the hold our Ego has on our lives.

 ## FAITH YOUR FEAR

Are the needs of others an afterthought? Or do you love to give but have trouble receiving? When we cleave to one principle over the other, we throw our life out of balance.

The Cycle of Life is based on interdependence. All lifeforms - trees, insects, fish, animals and humans - rely upon another, if, for nothing else, then for nourishment. One creature dies so another can live. It's "giving and receiving" in its purest form.

Selfish tendencies are easy to spot. We are preoccupied with our own interests at the expense of others. But rarely do we address the Egoic control of the givers who will not allow themselves to receive. The benevolence of giving is diminished when we reject the generosity of others. In doing so, we create a superior-subordinate relationship rather than one in which one party feels the joy of giving while the other experiences the vulnerability that comes from needing and allowing themselves to be taken care of.

 ## BE INSPIRED
Eyerusalem Mesele

Ever since I was a little girl, I've always been a "giver." Growing up, I did not think there was anything wrong with that; in fact, I thought it was an honorable trait. It was not until I got into my first relationship that I realized there is such a thing as giving too much, especially when you are also someone who has difficulty receiving. Through life's lessons and Tracey Knight's teachings, I've learned that to give without receiving is one of the greatest disservices you can do to your higher self. Coach Tracey taught me to "Let God love you through other people." As I allowed myself to feel and to know Love, I was able to give to others in a way I never thought I could. Now, in all my relationships I allow others to love me and give as I give to them. I am breaking the generational cycle of women who felt like they are undeserving of love.

 **PRACTICE SELF-MASTERY**

LEARN TO GIVE

If you need to strengthen your giving muscle, you must overcome the fear of not having enough. Stinginess, greed, gluttony, obsession, and hoarding comes from the belief in lack and limitation. It is a demonstration that you do not trust your Higher Power to provide for you abundantly.

The daily practice is to put yourself in situations where you have to trust your Higher Power to provide.

If you tend to buy too many groceries because you fear not having enough to eat, start buying only what is needed for a meal or two. The refrigerator may appear bare but remind yourself that life is generous.

Next, consider giving your "last" to someone in need. Remind yourself that you are participating in the Cycle of Life and as you give, you free yourself to receive.

LEARN TO RECEIVE

If you need to strengthen your receiving muscle, the resistance is to feeling vulnerable. Put yourself in situations where you have to ask for support, accept someone's generosity or be cared for by another. Be attuned to how you feel throughout the experience. Identify heavy feelings like guilt or shame and try to identify the reason why. Share your feelings in a journal and with a trusted confidant. Anything that is acknowledged has a better chance of being healed. Remind yourself that this is a part of the Cycle of Life and it's your Higher Power showing up to lend you support through a person or situation. Acknowledge your progress and humbly give thanks to the other person. Repeat the process often.

 AFFIRM YOUR INTENTION

- I give and receive generously from the storehouse of the Universe.
- There is no lack or limitation in my life. Freely, I give.
- I am safe. I am loved. I am divinely provided for.

 PRACTICE SELF-CARE

- Select a self-love activity from the back of the book to practice for 40 days.

Self-Mastery Principle # 11
To Know Freedom, Travel Light
and K.I.S.S. (Keep It Simple, Sweetie).

 **PONDER THIS**

Bigger isn't better and excess isn't affluence.

 FAITH YOUR FEAR

Life is simple and we are happier when we honor this truth.

We are conditioned to believe that the more we have the more secure we feel. We chase more money to feel financially safeguarded against poverty but the harder we work, the poorer our quality of life. We purchase bigger dwellings in which to store and protect our stuff but the more space we acquire, the more we have to buy to fill it. The more we own the more insecure we become about losing it. In our quest to be free and secure, we have inadvertently created a self-imposed prison.

Let go. Simplify and travel light. It's not our "stuff" that makes life worth living. The things that bring us true joy are found in the simple things – time to our self, experiences with loved ones, appreciating nature, watching children play - that cause us to lose track of time (and worry). Set yourself free of attachments to people, places or things and you shall know the protection and abundance that can only be provided by Spirit.

 **BE INSPIRED**
Clinton Clark

Most children begin life with the protection and security of one or both parents; I did not. I longed for the comfort of a traditional household but was reared by my paternal grandparents. They were loving but could not fill the void I felt. My grandmother told me very early on that I had to free myself from the bondage of my desire and accept reality. But she also assured me that I could still know love, peace and joy if I went within and kept life simple. She encouraged me to cultivate a strong relationship with the God of my own understanding and to use my faith as a lifeline. I could not afford a lot of missteps because I didn't have anyone to bail me out. What emerged was a simplistic but devoted lifestyle driven by necessity rather than excess. I apply these principles to every area of my life – not just material possessions. Emotionally, I travel light by being honest with myself and quickly letting go and forgiving others. Mentally, I travel light by staying positive and accepting reality – just like my grandmother advised. My goal is to keep life simple, avoid unnecessary burdens and allow my Higher Power to guide me. What began as a perceived deficit has turned out to be the blessing of freedom.

PRACTICE SELF-MASTERY

ACTIVITY 1:

A little at a time, begin to assess areas of your life where you can minimize and purge excess (i.e. clothes and other material possessions, items from the past, things you hope to use "one-day," food in the refrigerator, old resentments against others, and excessive goals). As you tackle each space, ask yourself, "What is necessary for me to live today?"

Affirm that your safe haven comes from within and not from the outside. Ask, "Why am I holding on? What type of "false security" (i.e. physical, mental, emotional, or spiritual) is this providing me? Next, ask yourself, "How do I create that same sense of safety in other ways?"

For example, if you feel financially insecure, you can create security by being more fiscally responsible through budgeting, investing and focusing on valuable assets that are not monetary in nature. If you are holding on to items from the past and find it difficult to get rid of them, examine the emotional attachments. Are you holding on to the illusion of a relationship or a feeling of loss? Did the relationship make you feel wanted, valued or loved? Focus on healing the wounds and becoming more emotionally available to heal existing relationships or establish new ones.

ACTIVITY 2:

Look for the simple treasures of life. What every day experiences make you laugh and/or feel joyful and abundant?

 AFFIRM YOUR INTENTION

• I take only what is needed and leave the rest.
• I look for the simple treasures of life.
• The closer I get to "me" the richer I become.

PRACTICE SELF-CARE

• Select a self-love activity from the back of the book to practice for 40 days.

Self-Mastery Principle # 12
Fear Can't Live Where Courage Reigns.

 PONDER THIS

From tiny acorns spring mighty oak trees. The question is, what type of seeds are you nurturing and growing in your garden?

 FAITH YOUR FEAR

We hold fears that were planted because of experiences (real or imagined) or the fear-based beliefs that have been passed down or shared by others. Our Humanness is protective. It wants to keep us safe and ensure our long-term survival. It uses fear to keep us out of harm's way even if that means keeping our goals at bay. When we allow our mind to cleave to the possibility of what could go wrong, we become stagnant and place a stranglehold on our success. Fear is like a weed growing wild in the garden of our life. The more we ignore it, it grows deep and spreads to every area of our life. It hinders our confidence, development and resilience. In order to free our lives from the grip of fear, we must plant different seeds - seeds of courage. Courage is not the absence of fear. It is being brave enough to unearth and heal pain and grief. It is the strength and will to forge a new way in the face of the unknown. Courage is an act of self-love that builds our character with Conviction, Integrity, Kindness, Willpower, and Action.

When these self-perpetuating seedlings are nurtured through practice, they enrich the soil of the soul and create an environment where we can heal and grow in unimaginable ways.

 **BE INSPIRED**
   Mahogany Taylor

Being a woman in a man's world isn't as seductive as one may think, particularly when construction is your livelihood and you aren't welcomed with open arms. Well that's exactly what I've faced being a woman in a male-dominated industry. Unwarranted doubt, judgement, double standards are ripe and fertile soil for fear, intimidation and self-doubt. How do you resolve being afraid to embrace and step freely into the thing that brings you peace, joy and fulfilment?

I had to make a choice. Stay where you are, listen to the rhetoric of the negative thoughts in my head "you aren't a man", "you can't be a general contractor or a builder", "you don't know how", "what if you fail," "nobody will hire you", "the men won't respect you" and be paralyzed by fear. Or remind myself who I am and what I'm capable of. Sometimes you must realign your thoughts and intention and press each moment, each day to overcome that fear. With each pressing it begins to dissipate as you feel and become more courageous. Remember, fear cannot live where courage reigns!

 **PRACTICE SELF-MASTERY**

ACTIVITY 1:

There are 8 simple steps to gardening. We will apply that same process to our emotional garden.

Step 1: Identify a good location. Select an area of your life where fear has reigned. What is your deepest fear in this area? Write it in the journal.

Step 2: Plan the layout of your garden. Decide what you want. Take a moment to sit quietly and create a detailed vision of your ideal state. Now feel it. What high vibration feelings come up for you? Wrap up this step by documenting in detail your vision and feelings in your journal.

Step 3: Till the soil to mix in organic matter, helps to control weeds and break up and loosen crusted areas. Now go back to what has been identified as your deepest fear. In your journal, write about the following: (a) What is the underlying belief that you hold about yourself? (b) Where did it come from? (c) How has it impacted your life? and (d) It is time to make a decision. Are you ready to change? Are you willing to give up pain in exchange for power – hurt for healing?

Step 4: Test the pH (acidity or alkalinity) of the soil to determine the level of toxicity. Will it produce plants that are rich in nutrients, or deficient in them? Disease flourishes in acidic environments, while alkaline conditions are conducive to health. The acidic effects of fear must be transmuted by the alkalinity of courage. As fear begins to die off, it may trigger the uncomfortable feelings and old habits that are a part of the Cycle of Grief – *Denial, Anger, Bargaining, Depression, and Acceptance.* Denial is pretending or longing for something different in the face of reality. Anger is resistance and may cause us to try and find fault. Bargaining is a clever attempt to negotiate new terms and conditions to avoid the inevitable. Depression is sadness and sometimes wanting to settle for less than we deserve. We go through these stages in no specific order and sometimes have to repeat certain steps until we surrender. Acceptance is agreeing to move forward and trusting the process. This leads to freedom to move, rather than remaining stuck. Get attuned to where you may be in this cycle and write about how it is standing in the way of your growth.

Step 5: Add what is needed to fill in the gaps and replenish the soil. Change does not have to take a long time; in fact, it can happen in an instant. Take time to create and practice affirmative statements that remind you to do the following: replace *Denial* with confirmation that it is time to change and you are ready for it; heal *Anger* by offering grace and forgiveness to yourself for being where you've been (we are always doing our best, but as we know better, we must do better); realize that the only *Bargain* needed is to swap hurt for healing and pain for powerfulness; release the feeling of being *Depressed* by looking to what you will gain, rather than what you will lose, through this transformation; and, give thanks as you *Accept* your new way of being.

Step 6: Plant Your Seeds. Courage is being brave with Conviction, Integrity, Kindness, Willpower, and Action. Go back to your vision and put an actionable plan in place. Use the characteristics of Courage to support you in the execution.

Step 7: Tend to your garden and watch it flourish. As you move through the process, support your efforts by revisiting Steps 5 and 6.

Another way to do this is through symbolism.

ACTIVTY 2:

Transfer and utilize this reflective energy by planting a peace lily or some other desired plant into a pot. Planting this indoor plant, nurturing it, watering it and speaking positivity over it will help build the habit and need to do the same for yourself. Name the plant. Decide where in your house it will thrive, and what you will need to do to ensure its survival. *Listen, you have the power of life in your own hands*. Despite how you've felt before, you get to decide how you nurture life for the plant, and for yourself.

 AFFIRM YOUR INTENTION

- I have the power of life in my own hands.
- Fear is nothing more than "False Evidence Appearing Real."
- Courage conquers all.

 PRACTICE SELF-CARE

- Select a self-love activity from the back of the book to practice for 40 days.

Self-Mastery Principle # 13
Forgiveness Cures the Poisonous Effects of Anger and Guilt.

 PONDER THIS

When you are bitten by a spider or snake, the poison sets up in the body and causes swelling, nausea and pain in the affected area. The longer it sits, unattended to, the sicker you become. The toxins slowly seep into the bloodstream, causing harm to the organs, paralysis and even death. Anger and Guilt have the same effect on the mental and emotional bodies. These intoxicating venoms can be subtle, like being annoyed or remorseful, or overwhelming, such as rage or depression. In either case, when they are ignored and left to fester in the dark, they morph into unyielding Resentment and Shame. Resentment and Shame are hardened forms of their counterparts. More importantly, they are the silent killers of happiness and self-love. Have you been bitten by the bugs of Anger or Guilt? What nauseating pain are you allowing to wreak havoc and steal your life?

 FAITH YOUR FEAR

Have you been disrespected, manipulated or subjected to violence or abuse? Were you abandoned, betrayed or deceived in your past and you never got over it? These experiences often create feelings of Anger and Guilt.

Guilt is the feeling of behaving out of alignment with your authentic self. Anger is a normal response to painful experiences. To feel is to be human but we are not meant to hold on to emotions lest they influence our personality and how we operate in the world. The effects of Anger and Guilt can be very subtle but significantly impact our ability to fully trust and love ourselves and others. Anger creates a data/information loop that the subconscious mind replays over and over and is then manifested in real experiences. In other words, you create your reality. A good indicator that Anger and Resentment are defining your character and experiences is when your M.O. is to be sarcastic, skeptical, critical, hostile, jealous, hateful, selfish or distant in any area of your life and relationships. Naturally, you will create encounters and interactions with people who reinforce that data loop.

If you want to be free to be happy, choose to heal. Begin by recognizing the source of the anger. If the incident is in the present, this will be a good time to apply the 6:24 Rule, which determines how much time you need to process and the best course of action (See the preface for a step-by-step guide). The Rule gives you 6 seconds to become self-aware of how you feel and to choose an empowering response. If you need more time, allow yourself up to 24 hours to take a time out. You can temporarily change your environment or avoiding talking to or about the person or situation so that you can gather your composure. The timeout is designed to allow your Humanness to feel what it feels. You can be the victim, villainize other parties, or just vent to a trusted friend who will listen without trying to solve your problem. Be intentional about letting them know what you need from them. At the end of the timeout period, it's time to get to work processing the pain, releasing grudges and finding a viable solution. First you will need to clear your emotions so that you can reclaim your power and make a decision that is best for you, without the influence of ego. Clarity comes through relaxation techniques like deep breathing, mediation, journaling or yoga. In your reflective space, Spirit will reveal the truth (include any part that you may have played) as well as your next course of action. Next, make the decision to take full ownership of and cleanse your data loop through Forgiveness. Forgiveness is a purging process that heals our mental, emotional and physical bodies. Forgiveness does not mean that you condone a person's behavior. It just creates a space to clear residual effects of the incident so that it does not hold you hostage. Oftentimes we need to forgive ourselves as much as others because we may feel as though we did not adequately protect, stand up for or love ourselves enough in the situation. If resentment is deep-seated, we may have to practice our forgiveness tool several times before it takes hold and we feel the relief. But with steadfast commitment, we will begin to heal and reclaim our power without the burden of Anger or Resentment.

BE INSPIRED
Angelus Ellis

When I think of forgiveness, I break it into two parts: forgiveness of self and forgiveness of others. I have had issues with both, with some successes and some setbacks. Here is one of my successes. After high school I went straight to college, as many do. The first year went well, but due to some drastic changes in my life, I ended up dropping out by my third year. That was 1993…and for many years after that I had a plethora of excuses as to why I didn't return, accompanied by a healthy dose of guilt and anger. Guilt about feeling inadequate compared to others I knew who did graduate. Anger from knowing I was just as intelligent as they were but lacked the trappings of a degree. But after some soul-searching, I realized that I wasn't angry at those people; I was *afraid* they were better than me. I was also afraid that if I went back I would stumble and fail again. At some point I had an epiphany: in continuing to make excuses and blaming the circumstances that led to me not completing my degree, I was still preventing me from getting my degree! This led to the realization that I had never forgiven myself for the mistakes I had made. This realization was like a weight lifting off my shoulders. Forgiving myself took work, but once I did, I understood that these so-called "mistakes" were actually lessons. I realized it took much less energy to walk back into college than it took for me to make excuses to stay out. When I forgave myself and let go of the anger and guilt, things with school fell in place like they never had before. I am proud to say I am looking at a 2020 graduation date. Masters after that….

There are two forms of forgiveness. Forgiveness of self and forgiveness of others. Sometimes forgiveness of self is the more difficult to do.

PRACTICE SELF-MASTERY

Ho'oponopono is an ancient Hawaiian practice of reconciliation and forgiveness. It was used by Dr. Ihaleakala Hew Len, a psychologist who cured every patient in the criminally insane ward of a Hawaii State Hospital without seeing a single one of them. Ho'oponopono is a cleaning tool that goes into the subconscious mind to purge the old data/information that is triggering low vibration feelings (i.e. anger, shame, guilt, etc.) and incidents in our lives.

The English translation of the word is "correction" or "to make right," thus empowering us to take full responsibility for every experience we create /call forth and heal it from the inside out, rather than focusing our energy and attention on people and circumstances that are outside of us.

Ho'oponopono can be practiced whether we are angry at a specific person or circumstance or have an anger issue that is obscure or difficult to pinpoint. As we go through this process it may trigger several inward questions; however, this is just resistance. Just be committed to a pure intention to own what you have created and surrender without judgment against yourself or others. When you hold this intention and go through the four simple but powerful steps below, Ho'oponopono becomes a tuning fork to elevate your vibrational frequency.

STEP 1: Repentance;

ACTION: State, "I'm Sorry." RATIONALE: As masters of our lives, we take full responsibility for EVERY thought and circumstance, even if it seems to be "out there," or caused or controlled by others. If we are experiencing it, we are responsible energetically for creating it. This is not about blame but about reminding ourselves that it's all for the purpose of our growth. With this in mind, let the anger-triggering experiences of your life illuminate your internal pain-points and be committed to healing without emotionally shutting down. When you own it, you don't have to wait on anyone else. You have the power to receive the lesson and heal yourself.

STEP 2: Forgiveness

ACTION: State, "Please forgive me" over and over, and mean it. RATIONALE: You don't need to know who you are asking for forgiveness, or for what reason. This is an opportunity to make amends for any and all data memories that include judgment, anger and resentment, thereby freeing yourself and others.

STEP 3: Gratitude

ACTION: State, "Thank You."

RATIONALE: Again, it does not matter who you are thanking. Thank God for awareness, your body for serving you. Thank yourself for being courageous or being you. Just be in gratitude.

STEP 4: Love.

ACTION: State, "I Love You." RATIONALE: Allow yourself to feel what it feels like to give and receive love. Hold that state of being by repeating it over and over.

AFFIRM YOUR INTENTION

- I am always doing the best I can in the moment…and that's enough.
- I forgive all things past…I forgive all things present…I forgive all things future.
- I trade guilt for goodness. I am a good person. I trade anger for peace. I am free.

♥ PRACTICE SELF-CARE

- Select a self-love activity from the back of the book to practice for 40 days.

Self-Mastery Principle # 14
Stop Hitting Myself… Stop Hitting Myself….
Stop Hitting Myself… with Self-Judgment.

 PONDER THIS

Judgment and criticism are forms of self-abuse. Moreover, when we judge ourselves, we can't help but to inflict that mistreatment on others as well. It's time to stop being so hard on yourself!

 FAITH YOUR FEAR

To judge is to disapprove of and condemn; what follows is disparaging statements that make us feel like we are always wrong or falling short. There is no way for us to give our best or persevere in the face of failure when the watchful eye of self-judgment looms overhead. Criticism is the byproduct of measuring ourselves against social norms. We must remember that all human beliefs and patterns came out of the mind of a man and no one person has the answer book on life. It is not until we begin to accept "who we are" as being "good enough" and that we are doing the best we can in the in the moment that we can step into the life we desire. In the areas that we want to improve, we commit to learn, practice and grow. We don't have to get it all right or be a perfect specimen in order to be accepted. We can choose to accept ourselves right now – today. As we love the totality of who we are, we will soon be able to accept others for who they are.

 **BE INSPIRED**
Andrea Garcia

How can my love for others be authentic when I do not love myself unconditionally? How can I truly forgive others when I do not know how to forgive myself? How can I truly relax and be at ease when I am constantly judging myself for all I have and have not done? How much is enough to take in or to give? Can I take a stand for myself? Very often I would disregard the subtleties of my own self-hatred; I allowed it to run the show as if every self-condemning thought was the truth. I often pushed through any circumstance without honoring my most basic needs, completely unaware of how deprived I had allowed myself to become. I realize now that I was disconnecting myself from my own experience and projected myself into the fixated thoughts on how I saw others' experiences. This was a way of perpetuating self-hating behavior. I finally got to the point where it was time to become aware of my own doing. I was creating my own experience without even knowing it. I had to take ownership of my own creation. As I began to take time for and with myself, to honor my needs and wants and to listen to that voice that was constantly whispering words of self-judgment, I could feel the pain that the voice was trying to share. As I listened, I could see how giving my power away to the thoughts and beliefs that "I am not enough" was robbing me of any sense of wellbeing. The solution for me was not more self-condemnation. It is not about judging myself for judging myself. The answer came when I answered the question, "To whom am I trying to prove my worth?" Answering this question allowed me to

43

reconnect with self and become present to my truth in the moment, which in turn gave me the opportunity to honor and empower myself. It was in this moment that I found my greatest feelings of release, contentment and peace.

 # PRACTICE SELF-MASTERY

There is a funny meme of a person using his own arm to hit himself while saying,

Stop Hitting Yourself…Stop Hitting Yourself…Stop Hitting Yourself!

This image is a commentary on self-judgment.

ACTIVITY 1:

Daily Practice: Whenever you notice yourself criticizing or comparing yourself to who you think you should be, create a vision in your mind's eye of you taking your own fist and hitting yourself over and over.

Ask yourself, "How ridiculous is it to hit myself in the head with critical thoughts and words?" Say, "I love myself too much to abuse myself in this or any way. In this moment, I am enough. I don't have to be perfect. I am perfect in my imperfections. I love and approve of myself as I am today." Repeat this statement over and over until you feel more centered. Then begin the process of deciding how you can best support yourself through whatever task or experience that triggered the ridicule.

ACTIVITY 2:

Daily Practice: It's time to hold yourself accountable for investing in yourself. Get a clear pitcher with a lid, preferably glass. Place a label on it that says, Quest to Invest in Me. Establish the rules: Every time you criticize, speak negatively or harm yourself with words or thoughts, you place $1 in the container. If you can afford it use a higher denomination (i.e. $5). You want the stakes to be high enough that you can see the impact of your words. At the start of the 40 days, get $20 in singles out of the bank in cash. That way you have it on hand. Acquire more singles as needed throughout the 6 weeks. At the end of each week, tally and record in your journal how much you had to contribute to the investment account. In the beginning, you will likely be investing a great deal. As time goes on, you should see less of a cash investment in the jar and more of an emotional investment in your well-being. Note your progress and be intentional about reframing your thoughts and language about yourself (and others).

At the end of the 40 days, total up the investment and deposit the money into a savings account. This will allow you to experience both a financial and emotional savings - a double bang for your buck. Cha-Ching!

 # AFFIRM YOUR INTENTION

- I love and approve of myself as I am today.
- The verdict is in: I am good enough!
- I see only beauty in myself and others.

 # PRACTICE SELF-CARE

- Select a self-love activity from the back of the book to practice for 40 days.

Self-Mastery Principle # 15
Comparison and Competition Steal Your Joy.

 PONDER THIS

Question: What, outside of yourself, do you truly have control over?

 **FAITH YOUR FEAR**

Competition and comparison are forms of control and an indicator that we are not secure with ourselves. To compare is to measure who you are and what you have/do against another. We note the differences and wonder if "what we have" or "who we are" is good enough to win at life. Deep down, we don't want to be left out or behind, so we begin to compete to make ourselves better than the other or to diminish their light and value. In either case, we lose. We fail to appreciate our uniqueness and then exert an inordinate amount of energy focused on trying to change our differences, which is something we cannot control. We create emotional and physical barriers that keep us from giving and receiving love and we increase our feeling of emptiness and isolation. In short, we miss out on the joy of being who we are and are unable to appreciate others. That said, some of us are naturally competitive. This is a gift that must be directed inward, as it can fuel our drive to be a better version of ourselves. Drop the need to rival against anything but who you were yesterday. Every day is an opportunity to create a better version of you.

 **BE INSPIRED**
Tracey Knight

I never saw myself as a competitive person. While I am kind and generous and I do a great job of supporting others, I did not know that my drive to be perfect and make everything "right" created an air of competitiveness among the people I loved and worked with. It wasn't until I started working on myself that I realized I had been comparing my achievements with those of others. Although I was sincerely happy and supportive of who they were and what they could do, I coveted anything I thought would make me better, not realizing that it wasn't meant for me to have "everything." More importantly, I was so busy comparing what I had and did not have, focusing on my perceived shortcomings, and trying to be like others that I was missing out on my own greatness. Through my everyday quest to love myself more, I have grown to appreciate my own unique qualities and experiences – whether others like them or not. I also realized that I *am* naturally competitive, but that this too is a good thing if directed in the right direction – inward. Today, I do not compete for attention or to be liked/better than someone else; instead, my only goal is to be better than I was the day before. Since I am a work in progress, I do sometimes revert to comparing myself to others, but now I am able to catch myself before it goes too far. What follows is the reminder of "What is for me, is for me," and "Who I am is good enough."

PRACTICE SELF-MASTERY

ACTIVITY 1:

Do a S.W.O.T. (Strengths, Weaknesses, Opportunities, Threats) inventory.

Cite your **Strengths**. When you do this, be generous and kind to yourself. If you have trouble, consider taking the Strength Finder Inventory on the I AM Tracey Knight website. For a nominal fee, you will use a statistically validated tool to uncover strengths you did not know you had. The tool will also share how to utilize these strengths in your career and daily life.

Knowing your **Weaknesses** is one of the most valuable tools you can possess. This is where you come to grips with the totality of who you are. Use this list to start confronting and working on overcoming your limitations. Each time you conquer a weakness, you overcome a fear and get emotionally stronger. This is about progress, not perfection. You just keep chipping at it with no predetermined endpoint.

Opportunities: List how your strengths and weakness can create an abundance of opportunities for you.

Threats: Identify the pitfalls of playing only to your strengths and ignoring your weaknesses. How do you lose?

Next, imagine you overhear people you work with (i.e. in a professional, community or volunteer setting) talking about you. Write about some of the things you'd want to hear them say about you, your strengths and shortcomings and your growth. What would you not want them to say about you?

ACTIVITY 2:

Take time each day to check in with yourself. When do you feel insecure? This is a key indicator that you are comparing yourself to someone or something, including a standard or belief that was set by others.

How has comparing yourself to others effected your relationships? Your self-worth?

Remind yourself that you are good enough, you have no control over people, places or things, and you are running your own race.

Next, play a game with yourself. As often as possible, find two things that fall under the same category and compare their differences and similarities. Explore their value and contribution. Take, for example, apples and oranges. Both are sweet fruits, yet they look, smell and taste very different. You would list their qualities and pinpoint that the apple is very good for digestive health, while the orange is good for the immune system. Each is valuable but plays a different role. Play this game with cars, houses, insects and animals, skillsets, etc. Finally, revisit your SWOT and enjoy exploring what you offer to every situation. The goal is to see the value in individuality and to replace judgment with appreciation.

ACTIVITY 3:

Watch the movie "Secretariat." Set in the 1960s, it's about a woman who found the courage and power to run her own race against all odds... and win.

AFFIRM YOUR INTENTION

- I'm running my race and I let others run their race.

- There is no competition or comparison. I am who I am and that is good enough.

- I look at myself as divinely created. My strengths, shortfalls, talents and abilities are neither better nor worse than anyone else's. They simply make me uniquely me.

 PRACTICE SELF-CARE

- Select a self-love activity from the back of the book to practice for 40 days.

Self-Mastery Principle # 16
Attitude of Gratitude!

 PONDER THIS

Which practice makes you feel better– complaining or expressing gratitude?

 FAITH YOUR FEAR

How do you spend most of your day – being sarcastic, cynical and wanting more, or in wonder, appreciation and contentment? Yes, there is always more to be had, but in order to win at being ourselves we must also value where we stand now and the journey that we took to get here. We have come so far, yet many of us never really take the time to stop, give thanks and recognize our growth. Additionally, life is only lived in the present moment. How many times have we been with family or friends and failed to relish the experience? How many times have we taken for granted the fact that we can see, taste, talk, walk, hear, think, speak or smell? When was the last time you looked on in wonder at a baby's curiosity and resilience or the awe-inspiring presence of nature?

There is so much to be thankful for in life. Gratitude puts us in a state of humility and it only requires our recognition and appreciation. Gratitude is giving the Divinity a high-five or a thank-you note for all that is given onto us.

 **BE INSPIRED**
   Bridgette Sears

Gratitude is my Attitude!! About fifteen years ago I decided that whenever someone asked me how I am, I would respond with "Grateful" as a reminder that I have so much to be grateful for in my life. The responses to this are both varied and Interesting. Some laugh, some say, "What a wonderful response!", and others ask what I am grateful for. I think they are shocked when I happily and enthusiastically give them a full-fledged list: I awakened this morning, I can walk, talk, hear, see, taste, touch, smell, think, feel, remember, breathe on my own, and do many other things someone somewhere is unable to do today, but for some reason, I can. I live in a space of gratitude, and when - as all of us do - I am having a moment of negativity, I quickly hear my spiritual team remind me to step back into gratitude because being grateful brings more things to be grateful for, even amidst what I perceive to be turmoil or chaos in my life. Living by this principle has added pure joy and happiness to my energy field; sometimes the feeling of gratitude is so powerful, I feet total giddiness throughout my body.

I feel the call to encourage others to be in this spiritual space as well. When others who are having a difficult time tell me they have nothing to be grateful for, I help them find reasons to be grateful. I ask them, "Didn't you awaken this morning?" and they say yes. I ask if they can hear and when they tell me yes, I tell them about a student I had who was wearing bilateral hearing aids and losing more of her hearing. Next, I remark on their ability to talk. I used to work with a student who was losing his ability to speak and would have to learn sign language as a means of communication. I then tell them of another student who was blind, and others unable to walk. I typically end with telling them how my aunt lived with the assistance of oxygen for 25 years, but they are able to breathe on their own. Many agree that they too have so much to be grateful for even if things aren't "perfect" or "ideal" in their lives.

 PRACTICE SELF-MASTERY

ACTIVITY 1:

Before you open your eyes in the morning and get out of bed, think of and affirm 10 different things you are grateful for.

ACTIVITY 2:

- For 40 days, tell one person why you are grateful for them.
- Stretch yourself to see the value in every experience and person by sharing that sentiment with a couple of people who trigger or irritate you.
- Be genuine in your acknowledgement.
- Consider putting a gratitude jar on your home counter or work desk with small cards next to it to.
- Encourage others to share their gratitude.

ACTIVITY 3:

Write a handwritten letter to someone who is not physically with you due to distance, death or conflict. Once you finish the letter, go to a place in nature. Read it aloud and then burn it.

ACTIVIY 4:

At least one day each week, sit quietly for 15 minutes in meditation. Visualize yourself in a sacred place talking with the Higher Power of your own understanding. Share all things you are grateful for in your life and in your relationship with Him/Her/It.

AFFIRM YOUR INTENTION

- I am grateful for the simple things in life.
- Life gives me so much joy and abundance.

 PRACTICE SELF-CARE

- Select a self-love activity from the back of the book to practice for 40 days.

Self-Mastery Principle # 17
Find Strength in Vulnerability.

 PONDER THIS

Contrary to what we have been taught, vulnerability is not weakness; it's strength.

 **FAITH YOUR FEAR**

Google the word vulnerability and you will find several definitions, including "weak," "defenseless," "helpless," and "susceptible to attack." It's enough to make any goal-driven person do whatever he/she can to avoid being or appearing vulnerable. No one wants to be in a position where they cannot take care of or protect themselves from harm. Another word used to define vulnerability is "openness." What dictionaries and search engines fail to acknowledge, however, is that the only way for us to know love and be intuitively guided by our Higher Power is to be open. An antonym of vulnerability is "resistant" – the implication being that one who is invulnerable is resistant to attack. The truth is when you are resistant you are guarded and missing out on the wisdom that comes with inspiration. To be inspired is to be "in-spirit." This is a state of true connection, love and knowing. But it is also the place where you can find the power to give and receive love without conditions.

True vulnerability has nothing to do with protecting yourself from other people – though the Ego-mind will try to convince you otherwise. It is about trusting the Divinity enough to surrender your intellect and what you think you already know (about everything) to receive and follow Its directions. This is called Faith. Faith is the practice of being vulnerable to your Spirit.

 **BE INSPIRED**
Kenya Simmons

For a long time, I confused vulnerability with weakness. This notion stemmed from constantly finding myself in emotionally trying situations and not knowing how to process them. As I grew older and cleared the muddy spaces in my life, a clear perception of myself began to form. I came to understand how my sensitivity manifested, the silence I forced upon it and the detriment it caused. Only after I spent an extended amount of time alone did I see how I relinquished my own power. I learned how trusting yourself one hundred percent gives your vulnerability its strength and how moving honestly with this strength gives your vulnerability power.

 **PRACTICE SELF-MASTERY**

ACTIVITY #1

Daily Practice: Trusting your own instincts makes space for you to be open and receptive. To become attuned, develop a regular practice (i.e. meditation, mindfulness, yoga, Qi Gong, Tai Chi or taking walks or sitting in nature) that allows you to hear the intuitive guidance of your Higher Power/Spirit. The goal is to turn down the chatter of your Humanness to hear the gentle, unassuming voice of Divinity. The practice(s) should be done daily to help you to stay attuned to what it feels like to be connected, loved and guided. You will also become comfortable with being vulnerable with your Higher Self. Begin to recognize how it speaks to you. Do you get a tingling or quickening in your body? Do you feel a certain way? Learn to go within and ask before acting or making a decision – big or small. Used consistently, these practices will provide clarity about how to move and, most importantly, help you summon the courage to do so.

ACTIVITY #2

Weekly Practice: To trust yourself, you must be yourself. If you fear how others will look at you or judge you, then you will be tempted to modify who you are to fit in around others. Modifying who you are or acting like a different person than who you really are is a sign that you feel uncomfortable and/or exposed being you.

Challenge yourself to be your most authentic self. For example:

- If you wear makeup or body enhancers, for the next 40 days, go without.
- If you're too embarrassed to flatulate (pass gas) or defecate in the house/ restroom when someone is there, openly acknowledge that you need to excuse yourself to engage in this normal, human bodily function.
- Illuminate a particular flaw or deficient skill publicly.
- If you have a silly laugh or sense of humor, share it publicly.
- If you are a person who is always in the company of others, practice being alone.
- Openly acknowledge your mistakes. Make amends where necessary and move on.
- Stand naked in front of the mirror for 15 minutes and revel in your beauty. Affirm your greatness.
- Go to lunch/dinner with someone who is not necessarily a friend and who has differing beliefs.

If you are accustomed to being one way at home and a different way in public, at work or in the presence of others, commit to showing the hidden side of yourself.

Consider it as a fast from your man-made self.

ACTIVITY 3:

Challenge yourself to participate in an activity that is safe, fun but requires you to trust Spirit (i.e. skydiving, rock climbing, ziplining, rafting, go carting, bumper cars).

AFFIRM YOUR INTENTION

- I surrender to the Divinity in me.
- I am open and receptive to following my instinct.
- I find strength in being vulnerable. I am always safe.

 PRACTICE SELF-CARE

- Select a self-love activity from the back of the book to practice for 40 days.

Self-Mastery Principle # 18
Be Still… Be Silent.

PONDER THIS

Seeds are planted in the stillness and darkness of the ground and they bloom. We spend nine months developing in the calmness of the womb. At night, we go to sleep, giving our bodies a chance to grow and rejuvenate. Why should our daily lives be any different if we want to flourish?

In the stillness and silence, you can hear all you need to know to optimize your life.

FAITH YOUR FEAR

Run, run, run! Busy, busy, busy! For many of us, life has become one long, chaotic to-do list. Our calendars are filled to capacity – oftentimes with things meant to support or impress others. We hurry through our day, sometimes neglecting to take the proper time to eat and rest; some of us even delay nature's call. We have become slaves to the cell phones and computers that were supposed to be our tools, and we can never seem to figure out "where the time went." When we live our lives outside of ourselves, we place importance on "doing," rather than "being." Each day becomes an endless checklist of tasks that have to be accomplished with very little fulfillment and never enough time or energy to complete them. Each moment comes and goes as a blur; and we wonder why we have trouble remembering what day it is or what we did the day before. We may even start to worry that we're suffering from a cognitive or emotional syndrome like dementia, Alzheimer's disease or clinical depression. More likely, it is the result of being "presently absent" in our lives. To course correct, we must create a new paradigm, one that includes "stillness." Stillness is this context is not just motionlessness, but the state of tranquility achieved through mindful silence. Mindfulness is the exercise of being present or aware. Silence is feeling the presence of and listening to the gentle voice of the Divinity. Thus, stillness is a ritual of setting aside or clearing out the chatter of your busy thoughts to consciously concentrate on the presence and guidance of your Higher Power. During this window of time, everything in life slows down, you become calm as you reflect inward. Given your usual state of busy-ness, this practice may initially feel uncomfortable. With persistence, however, this suspended state of serenity will miraculously provide everything you need in the way of clarity, strength and direction. You will begin to let go of what no longer serves you, prioritize what is important and see yourself in a new light that will increase your self-esteem and confidence. You will begin to live your life from the inside out.

BE INSPIRED
Kim Griffin

Still means deep silence and calm. Stillness is a place where I can hear clearly what's going on inside of me or see the beauty around me. Stillness is a place and a gift that allows me to act, not react. Stillness brings me balance. This is one of the ways I get to my still place. I take a seat in a quiet spot, take a deep breath and read each line, breathing in between each line.

Take a deep Breath

"Be Still and Know that I am God."

Breathe

Be Still and Know that I am…

Breathe

Be Still and Know that I…

Breathe

Be Still and Know that…

Breathe

Be Still and Know…

Breathe

Be Still and

Breathe

Be Still

Breathe

BE

PRACTICE SELF-MASTERY

There are several ways to practice stillness/mindfulness. Research a few and see what resonates with you. I suggest having more than one formal practice so that you can see how easy it is to incorporate stillness into several areas of your life.

Daily Practice: Begin with a minimum of 15 minutes of meditation. The best time to do this is before you start your day, though some people find it helpful to do it midday to center themselves and increase their energy. Meditation takes practice. In the beginning, you may become frustrated by the endless chatter in your head. No worries; this is normal. Experts say our mind thinks over 70,000 thoughts per day. That's around 3,000 thoughts per hour! That means thinking is habitual, and habits can be changed! When your mind wanders off and gets caught up in a memory loop, make it your goal to learn how to step over the distraction and come back to center.

Guided meditation, mantras, music, imagery, and even your own breath are all helpful tools in this regard. You may also want to get a strand of 108 mala or prayer beads, such as those used in Buddhist mediation, to count the number of times you recite a mantra or breathe while meditating. Hold the mala in your right hand, draped between your middle and index fingers. There should be a larger "guru bead" that may be positioned as a starting point. Each time you breathe or recite your mantra in your head or aloud, you pull the next, smaller bead toward you. You will repeat this process 108 times, traveling around the strand until you return to the guru bead. This will typically take about 12 to 15 minutes.

ACTIVITY 2:

Weekly Practice: Select another mindfulness experience to incorporate into your weekly schedule. Other practices include Yoga, Tai Chi, Qi Gong, walking in nature, deep breathing, and any other daily activities that are completed in a "mindful" manner. An example is brushing your teeth with complete and uninterrupted focus on that task. Then you move to making the bed, preparing your meal or taking a shower. The goal is to refrain from multitasking or engaging with other distractions (i.e. family members, TV, cell phone, etc.) during this timeframe.

 AFFIRM YOUR INTENTION

- I am present in my life.

- Breathe!

- God, grant me the serenity to accept the things that I cannot change, the courage to change the things I can and the wisdom to know the difference.

 PRACTICE SELF-CARE

- Select a self-love activity from the back of the book to practice for 40 days.

Self-Mastery Principle # 19
Let Go of the Fantasy and Live in Reality.

 **PONDER THIS**

Do you know the difference between fantasy and reality?

 FAITH YOUR FEAR

Wikipedia defines a story as "an account of imaginary or real people and events told for entertainment purposes." Every experience we have creates a memory that is stored in the subconscious mind. Before, during and after the encounter we form a perspective about it - "the story." If the experience was good, we may form a fanciful love story that affirms, over and over again, just how wonderful and enjoyable it was. If the experience was perceived as negative, the story becomes a "nightmare." Every subsequent experience then gets compared against it as either the gold standard or something to be avoided at all costs.

In the case of the love story, subsequent experiences oftentimes do not measure up. We then find ourselves constantly chasing this fictional account of how perfect he/she/ it was, only to be continuously disappointed. If we have experienced a nightmare, our tolerance for people and similar situations may become very low and we bail out at the first sign of a reoccurrence. Engaging in this fantasy life, positive or negative, prevents us from truly giving situations a wholehearted and resilient effort. It keeps us guarded and stands in the way of our experiencing and growing from life's valuable experiences. Every person we encounter and every situation we live through is there to teach us more about who we are. If we lean in and are willing to learn – regardless of whether the situation produces pleasant or unpleasant feelings – we get the lesson and become a stronger version of ourselves. This requires that we surrender the stories we've told ourselves and live in the reality of each event as it comes. We forgo comparing and contrasting to past memories (our own or others') and instead commit to seeing the value and opportunity in the moment, taking what is needed and leaving the rest.

 **BE INSPIRED**
Jennifer Bliss

We live, we choose, we learn, we grow. For me, this meant letting go of the fantasy that things could have been any different.

You see, I was married for twenty years and didn't want to get divorced, so I suppressed (ignored) all the warnings and instead opted to live the fantasy, celebrating the love I used to have rather than accepting the reality of what it had become. What I know now is that living in a fantasy can make you sick. It is a denial of life.

It wasn't until I let go of what I thought should happen and embrace what was actually happening that I began to let go and heal. It is unhealthy to accept sprinklings of attention and interaction to give our self the illusion of being loved, cared for and happy.

Sometimes we must let go of what is killing us, even though it's killing us to let it go.

 **PRACTICE SELF-MASTERY**

ACTIVITY 1:

Get two balloons, two note-card-sized pieces of paper and a pen. Identify one past experience that you are constantly trying to replicate and one you are trying to avoid.

What type of story have you told yourself about each thing? Write the positive occurrence on one piece of paper and the negative on the other. On the back side of each paper, identify the feelings that are attached to each occasion. Did the situation make you feel wanted or rejected? Did the experience seemingly build your self-confidence and the other deplete your life force? Did the situation(s) mimic the trials and heroic acts of a Grimm or Disney fairytale? Was there a villain to your victim?

Fold each paper into a small square or rectangle and insert it into one of the deflated balloons. Now, blow the balloons up enough so that they can float away, then tie them off and take them outside.

Acknowledge that these events happened. Share the lesson or value each one added to your life. Remember, keep the focus on you – not someone else making you a victim or causing you to act or fail to act in a certain way. Own your life.

As they float away, verbally give thanks for the experiences, then release the balloons into the ethers.

In your journal, apologize to yourself for using them as measurements for all subsequent events. Write about how you allowed those experiences to shape your behavior. Did you become stuck and stagnant in an area of life? Did you develop self-sabotaging habits? Did you become isolated or siloed (meaning you withhold information)? Are you afraid of relationships? Do you struggle with trusting yourself and others? Do you expect the worst from people? How did the experiences define your beliefs and language about yourself and others?

Acknowledge that each experience was but one incident in time. Make a commitment to no longer allow the past to define your future. Tell yourself how proud you are for taking this step to free yourself from fairytale stories. Next, make the commitment to take each event in your life as it comes and when the habit of referencing the old story comes up (and it will), remind yourself that you have released that pattern and this is a new day and a new experience and you are open to what it brings to your life.

ACTIVITY 2:

Identify other stories you are holding onto. Here are a few areas to consider:

*   Examine the stories you tell yourself about how your love interest is/was "supposed" to behave in relationship with you.

*   What story did you tell yourself about how your mother, father or caregiver was supposed to be compared to how they were in reality.

- What story do you tell yourself about what you are entitled to, based on your acquired (or lack of) education, status, title or means?
- Look for places in your life where you feel guarded or distant in your interactions. What story did you make up around why you need to behave in this manner?
- What stories do you have about your relationship with spending, earning or receiving money?
- Think about how you relate to a specific group of people (i.e. women). Are there any trust issues? If so, what stories are guiding how you interact with them?

Write out the story as you have portrayed it and then create a new narrative that reflects the truth.

Repeat the balloon exercise in Activity 1.

 AFFIRM YOUR INTENTION

- I seek and operate in the truth.
- I call "a thing" a thing.
- I stay in the present, allowing each new experience to stand on its own merit.

 PRACTICE SELF-CARE

- Select a self-love activity from the back of the book to practice for 40 days.

Self-Mastery Principle # 20
Stretch the Resistance and Expand Your Capacity.

 PONDER THIS

Do you have trouble staying consistent when you are working to kick a habit? Are you wondering why – despite your best efforts – you fall short of your intended goal? If so, you are facing that immortal enemy, Resistance.

 FAITH YOUR FEAR

Resistance is an internal battle to avoid change! The two opponents are the old and stagnant you and the new and progressive you. Clever, covert and stubborn, Resistance is the biggest opposition to expanding your capacity and achieving success. The truth is, everything on the planet is changing. We have no control over it. In fact, if you are not changing, you are not growing and if you are not growing, you are dying – and who wants to do that? Our Spirit has created an environment where change happens subtly. We went from being an embryo to a baby to a toddler effortlessly. We did not resist the transformation. It wasn't until we became adults that we began to resist everything – fighting against the natural flow of life. We don't want gray hair, so we color it. We hold on to relationships even when there are signs that we and/or our partner have grown in different directions. We are being asked to shift our spending habits and minimize our financial burdens, but we instead spiral down the path of destruction and indebtedness just to keep up appearances.

Our career is no longer fulfilling or we don't fit into the culture, but instead of gracefully finding a different role or organization, we hold on to the paycheck for dear life until we are fired, laid off or just cannot take the emotional weariness. These are all signs of resistance. Resistance is a common posture of our Humanness and it lives in the physical body. Ninety-five percent of how the body behaves is habitual. Remember, Humanness is committed to maintaining what is familiar and comfortable, even if the habits are injurious. Our thoughts and feelings, which feed each other, are the place where change begins or vegetates. If your thoughts and feelings are uncompromising, you will become rigid in your vision and outlook which in turn effects every other areas of your life (i.e. thoughts and feelings create your words; words create actions; actions create habits; habits create your character; character creates your destiny). This is known as suffering. As you can imagine, when you are in misery, your chances of expanding your capacity and fully living up to your potential is significantly diminished. It does take practice to get your Humanness to settle down and accept that not only is change inevitable, it is good for us.

Surrender is the only cure. To surrender means to let go and allow. It is a willingness to trust the process of learning and becoming something new, even though you are familiar and most comfortable with the old. Surrender is not weakness or an invitation to do nothing. It is an action word that does not require willful force. If you're one of the many people who ask, "How do you surrender?", know that this in and of itself is resistance. We don't have to know how – there is a power greater than ourselves that is in charge of that. We must simply be willing to relinquish the need to control. Remember, we are always safe to change when we trust and obey the intuitive guidance of Spirit.

 **BE INSPIRED**
   Schnavia Bronson

There was time when I came home nearly every day extremely frustrated from a job I "loved." Though I thoroughly enjoyed my work, I rarely felt as though my contributions were acknowledged, much less supported. I often sounded like a broken record as I divulged my workplace challenges to trusted friends and colleagues. I received all types of advice, mostly about how I didn't deserve that kind of treatment; I didn't know my own worth; and that I should go where my skills and talent would be appreciated. But the advice that resonated with me most was, "You can only do for people what they will allow you to do. If folks can't see what you see or refuse to be forward-thinking, it's okay, but don't let that stop you from being or giving your best. In this season, learn to be still, gain clarity and prepare for what's next. This is the time to sharpen your saw. Be intentional. Use this time to stretch yourself and learn new things. You said you wanted to go back to school, so go. Redirect your frustration into something that will ultimately benefit you. God will tell you when it's time for you to move on and when you do leave, you will be ready for that next place…you'll be ready for the next phase of your life journey." In that moment, I realized that my habitual state of frustration was a result of my resistance to growth. I was comfortable with where I was and confident in my skill set and abilities - or was I? To be completely honest, fear paralyzed me from actualizing my dreams. Thus, I tried desperately to be content with where I was and who I had become. Secretly, I wanted more but had no idea where to begin. That's why I was only able to focus on what I wasn't getting, rather than the opportunities staring me in the face. Like me, this is your season- your opportunity to Expand Your Capacity!

 **PRACTICE SELF-MASTERY**

ACTIVITY 1:

Where in your life are you stuck? Where do you feel like you are falling short of your goals or the vision for your life? What don't you want to change? What are you resistant to? Pinpoint one area of your life that feels stagnant and make the decision to confront the resistance that you are experiencing. Perhaps you want to improve your health but you are resistant to changing your diet or fitness routine. Examine your finances and ability to manage money, save or refrain from financing other people's poor habits. Maybe it's time to focus on your career or the business you have been wanting to launch? What have you allowed to stand in the way of up-leveling? Many people want to experience a shift in their relationships. Are you resistant to opening up or letting go?

There is no single recipe for overcoming resistance. It's a work in progress but here are a few steps to support you in your daily practice:

* Become aware of what you are resistant to (typically, it's related to a fear of something). Oust it by acknowledging its presence.

* Make the commitment to become more flexible. Use Activity 2 to assist in with this. Physical flexibility leads to mental and emotional pliability.

* Use your resistance to your advantage (i.e. to reduce risk). Resistance can tell you where you need to develop a particular skill or heal an old wound, among other things. Look for what it is telling you and address it.

- Determine whether you are afraid of losing or succeeding or both. Get to the bottom of what is keeping you stuck. If you are afraid of failing, figure out how the failure can grow you or benefit you. You can also use the activities listed under Self-Mastery Principles related to fear, vulnerability and failure to help you overcome this barrier. If you are afraid of succeeding, ask yourself what it will mean if you succeed (i.e. more pressure, the need to be perfect). Remember, you are not living to please other people. Your success is for you.

- Get a coach. Sometimes we need an objective accountability partner to help us see our blind spots.

ACTIVITY 2:

Make a "T-chart," which is a side-by-side comparison similar to a pros and cons list. Down the left column, list all the ways this change will benefit you. In the right column, list how the change could be challenging for you. Next, come up with a viable solution to each challenge in the right column – even if it is just learning to accept that you are not always in control. Review your list to inspire growth and soothe your insecurities about change.

ACTIVITY 3:

Practice Surrender by reciting any of the following:

- Serenity Prayer

God, grant me the serenity to accept the things I cannot change, the courage to change the things that I can and the wisdom to know the difference.

- Unity Prayer

The light of God surrounds us;

The love of God enfolds us;

The power of God protects us;

The presence of God watches over us;

Wherever I am God is. Wherever others are (or this situation is) God is!

Wherever we are, God is!

ACTIVITY 4:

Yoga is the practice of connecting body with intention. When your body is stiff and rigid, it is a reflection of the beliefs and thoughts you hold about yourself, your life and others. What or who are you trying to control? Are you willing to expand your perception about how things "should" be? Where can you be more flexible?

Attend a yoga class or practice in your home. Set an intention around an area in which you want to grow but may be experiencing resistance. While practicing yoga, reach with your arms...extend your legs...bend your back... and be flexible in your thoughts and beliefs about who you are and what you can accomplish relative to the goal. See how the body responds. Talk to it and encourage it to change; explain why you need this change. Congratulate and affirm any success you achieve. Practice regularly.

ACTIVITY 5:

Look for situations, conversations, perceptions, viewpoints, biases, relationships, diet/taste buds or palate, experiences, and other areas of your life where you could stand to be more open, receptive or flexible. Open yourself up to listening, exploring and having conversations without debate.

It is perfectly okay to have an experience just for the sake of it. It does not mean you have to adopt a particular thought or behavior permanently. The choice is yours. Just having the experience will teach you something about yourself while stretching your capacity. Repeat this process at least one each day

 AFFIRM YOUR INTENTION

- I am flexible in all areas of my life.
- I am in flow.
- I surrender all.

 PRACTICE SELF-CARE

- Select a self-love activity from the back of the book to practice for 40 days.

Bonus Self-Love Principle
Food Is Fuel, Not a Lover.

 PONDER THIS

It's time to examine our relationship with food. Are we dating, married, divorced or having an *"it's complicated"* affair? Food is any nutritious substance that is consumed in order to grow and maintain one's life force. Food is not meant to be a sedative, coping mechanism for stress or a companion when our feelings and needs go unaddressed.

 FAITH YOUR FEAR

Our upbringing lays the groundwork for our relationship with food. For some of us, eating was a focal point. Upon rising and throughout the day, there may have been a discussion about when, where and what we would eat for each meal. Some parents withheld desserts and other special treats as a means of punishment for talking back or poorly performing on an assigned task. On the other hand, food may have been used as a reward if we did our chores or earned good grades. Perhaps the family singled out a regular day or event and used food as the acknowledgement (i.e. on payday we are treated to pizza). The most deep-seated behavior comes from the belief that buying, preparing (especially during the holidays) and eating excessive amounts of food are a display of wealth and prosperity. This idea may derive from either cherished cultural events or traumatic societal institutions such as slavery. In any case, our relationships with food began very early in our development. It is up to us to replace triggers and avoid perpetuating unhealthy, food-related obsessions, compulsions and disorders. In doing so, we will learn to relate to food for what it is, "a necessary and valuable resource that serves as a means-to-an-end."

 PRACTICE SELF-MASTERY

Meal Prep

Take your time. Prepare a healthy meal. As you eat it, savor the flavor and appreciate the benefits to your body.

Full of Cravings

Hunger is a need for the nourishment that provides energy to the mind and body. Cravings are chemical, hormonal or emotional signals that something is out of balance. Solution: For 40 days, consistently check in with yourself to determine whether you are truly hungry or if you're having a craving. If it is a craving, ask yourself what is it that you need in the moment (i.e. a physical or emotional break or acknowledgment). Are you afraid of something like going hungry, or is eating this food just a habit)? Use a food journal to track and become aware of when you crave certain foods. What are you doing or feeling during that period? What exactly are you craving? The type of food can tell you a great deal about your emotional state of being

(Constant Cravings by Doreen Virtue is an excellent resource). Find alternative ways of coping with the trigger (i.e. taking a walk; using perseverance to push through blocks and completing the task at hand by offering yourself a healthy, non-food related reward). Consider getting your hormones tested and continue to strengthen your emotional health.

The Shame of Eating Too Much

"One is too many and 1000 is never enough" is a saying used in 12-step recovery. There are those foods that trigger obsessive and compulsive tendencies (i.e. chips and sugary treats). We know as soon as we eat one we will not be able to stop and when we do, we are confronted with guilt for doing it and shame because we judge ourselves as weak-minded. Solution: As we work to unveil our emotional and biological triggers, we must put ourselves in situations where we will win. First, if you find yourself in an eating binge, try to use temperance. Next, recognize that guilt is a useful indicator that we are out of alignment with who we say we are. Know your triggers and avoid your weaknesses. When at the grocery store, don't even go down the aisle that contains the foods you crave. If you are in a room where those foods are present, don't take the first bite as it may activate the urge for more. If you are experiencing peer pressure, thank people for the offer but let them know that you have chosen a different lifestyle. Remind yourself of both the consequences and rewards of your choices. Remove yourself from any environment where the temptation is too great. Seek help from trusted family members, friends, coaches and support groups like Overeaters Anonymous. As we take the right course of action, any guilt we feel can be released. Shame, on the other hand, has no place in our lives. It is self-judgment (self-abuse), pure and simple, and a repeat of a process that no longer works for us. Instead, we must gift ourselves with grace, mercy and forgiveness as we shift.

 AFFIRM YOUR INTENTION

- I listen to my body and give myself exactly what is needed in the moment.
- Food is a source of fuel. I only eat when I am hungry.
- I reclaim my power as I create harmony with my thoughts, body, food.

 PRACTICE SELF-CARE

- Select a self-love activity from the back of the book to practice for 40 days.

Self-Care Principles

Self-Care Principle # 1
Find a "Peace" of Nature.

PONDER THIS

Did you know that nature offers a reset button to counter inner turmoil?

PRACTICE SELF CARE

Take a 20-minute walk and enjoy the calm, simplicity of nature.

AFFIRM YOUR INTENTION

Life is tranquil and so am I.

Self-Care Principle # 2
Topple the Tension.

PONDER THIS

Did you know that regular massages or a 20-minute bath once a week can help lower your stress levels?

Massage therapy is a manipulation of the body tissue. It releases tension, stagnant energy and helps get you moving in a new direction. Quite simply, massages revitalize and restore the body to its natural state of harmony.

PRACTICE SELF CARE

Get or give yourself a massage. Right before you go to bed tonight, use your favorite oil to give yourself a foot massage. Spend 10 minutes on each foot, paying careful attention to how relaxed and reinvigorated you feel afterward. If you want to have a professional experience, consider springing for a full-body Swedish massage, reflexology treatment, shiatzu or acupressure.

Round out your massage experience with a warm bath and your choice of bath salts and essential oils.

AFFIRM YOUR INTENTION

Relax, Relate, Rejuvenate.

Self-Care Principle # 3
Just Breathe!

PONDER THIS

Shallow or deep? Have you paid attention to your breath when you're under stress?

PRACTICE SELF CARE

Slowly and deeply breathe in for a count of 7…hold for 7…breathe out for 7. Repeat three times.

AFFIRM YOUR INTENTION

My breath is my life force. I take it in, in abundance.

Self-Care Principle # 4
Look for a Miracle.

PONDER THIS

What blessings are happening in your life, events you know you had little to no control over?

PRACTICE SELF CARE

Look for surprising and welcomed events, no matter how small.

AFFIRM YOUR INTENTION

Something miraculous is happening today.

Self-Care Principle # 5
Do a H.O.L.Y. Dance.

PONDER THIS

How often do you let go and dance in celebration of you?

Music is the language of the world. No matter what social, economic, cultural or language barriers might exist, music breaks through them all. Music penetrates and communicates with the soul.

PRACTICE SELF CARE

What does your soul need to hear right now? Find one of your favorite songs and let the music provide the therapy you need.

If you don't have a particular song you'd like to dance to, try H.O.L.Y. by Florida Georgia line. It stands for "High on Loving You!" Above all, don't worry whether you're "doing it right," just dance to your own beat!

AFFIRM YOUR INTENTION

Dance, dance, dance. Life is a joy.

I sing…I dance…I let the music elevate my life.

Self-Care Principle # 6
Play with Me!

PONDER THIS

Do you remember what it was like when you played as a child?

PRACTICE SELF CARE

Take yourself on a "playdate," enjoying simple games and activities.

AFFIRM YOUR INTENTION

I play with childlike wonder.

Self-Care Principle # 7
"Book" a Journey.

PONDER THIS

Need a trip but don't want to commit to the time away or the financial investment?

PRACTICE SELF CARE

Reading is a lost art. Take 30 minutes and let yourself get lost in the life and journey of the characters of a good book.

AFFIRM YOUR INTENTION

I let my imagination create beauty and joy in my life.

Self-Care Principle # 8
I Could use a Hug.

PONDER THIS

Want to build trust, elevate your mood and heal feelings of loneliness, isolation, depression and anger?

PRACTICE SELF CARE

Give yourself a loving hug. Wrap your arms around your body for 3 minutes. Enjoy the feeling of being embraced and intimate with yourself.

AFFIRM YOUR INTENTION

I give myself touches of love.

Self-Care Principle # 9
Every Day is a Day to Celebrate!

PONDER THIS

What are you waiting for? Why are you saving your "best" perfume, clothes, jewelry, fine china or wine for a special occasion? Each day is a blessing and a day of celebration.

PRACTICE SELF CARE

Take out and use the items you hold for special occasions or reward yourself with a treat – a hidden pleasure!

AFFIRM YOUR INTENTION

I "treat" myself well – every day!

Self-Care Principle # 10
Disconnect

PONDER THIS

In this fast-paced world of technology, we are always "online," always connected. And we wonder why we're so stressed?!

PRACTICE SELF CARE

Take a break. Detox from phones, technology and social media. Feel what it is like to be present in your life and relationships. Depending on your lifestyle and dependence on technology, you may have to start with small increments of time (i.e. an hour or two) and work your way up to a day.

AFFIRM YOUR INTENTION

Today, I am present.

Self-Care Principle # 11
Friendship is Good for the Soul.

PONDER THIS

Isn't life better when it is shared with others?

There are no strangers…only teachers. Every person you meet is a teacher. Every situation is an opportunity to grow.

PRACTICE SELF CARE

1. Have dinner with a friend. Listen…Share…Joke…Laugh…Enjoy!

2. Expand your circle. Be open to learning. Make it a point to meet someone new today.

AFFIRM YOUR INTENTION

I am a good friend and my life is enhanced through connection with others.

Self-Care Principle # 12
Get Up and Move!

PONDER THIS

There are so many people who are incapacitated. When was the last time you gave thanks through your actions for your whole, healthy and complete body?

PRACTICE SELF CARE

No excuses! Get up and move your body. Engage in at least 20 minutes of exercise (i.e. walk, run, aerobics, yoga, etc.). Give thanks that you are blessed with mobility.

AFFIRM YOUR INTENTION

My body is my temple and I honor it by stretching and moving it.

Self-Care Principle # 13
Clean Out the Clutter.

PONDER THIS

Are you holding onto the past? Our external environment mirrors our internal one; therefore, clutter is a sign that you may be resisting transformation in your life. Where do you have pockets or rooms of clutter or chaos?

PRACTICE SELF CARE

Take the first-step toward transformation. Clean out a drawer, your car, a closet. Make the commitment to let go of the "stuff" that no longer serves your greatest and highest good – in all areas of your life.

AFFIRM YOUR INTENTION

I am willing to let go.

Self-Care Principle # 14
Hydrate with an "Inside Shower."

PONDER THIS

Did you know that the human body is comprised of 60% water? It is used for elimination, cell generation, joint and organ and hydration. That makes water one of our most precious assets. Most of us take 1 or 2 showers or baths a day because we want to look and smell fresh. What about the inside? How clean are you?

PRACTICE SELF CARE

A rule of thumb for hydrating our body to drink half of our body weight in ounces each day. This will provide adequate fluid to clean and refresh our internal body.

AFFIRM YOUR INTENTION

Water does my body good.

Self-Care Principle # 15
Creative Expression.

PONDER THIS

Creativity is an outward manifestation of joy. Joy is a celebration of love and life! There are no rules for creative expression – it can look, feel or be voiced in whatever way makes you feel good. How do you say YES! to the joy of your life?

PRACTICE SELF CARE

Children are great role models when it comes to expressing joy and being creative. They have no expectations of or conditions on the finished product. Take a cue from them and find your way to creatively express your delight for how beautiful life really is (i.e. color, draw, sing, play an instrument, engage in a hobby or arts/craft, or anything that makes your heart sing with fulfillment).

AFFIRM YOUR INTENTION

My creativity is honored and expressed in unique ways.

Self-Care Principle # 16
Take a Catnap.

PONDER THIS

Chronic stress and overuse of technology are contributing to our sleep- deprived society. Yet, other than children and older adults, napping is frowned upon as a waste of time or a sign of laziness. This is not true! In fact, research shows that when we are rested we are much more alert and productive and have a better disposition. Sleep also provides an opportunity for the body to heal.

PRACTICE SELF CARE

When I don't snooze, I lose. No apologies or justifications needed. Take a 20- to 30-minute nap. No TV or technology. Just shut it all down and rest.

AFFIRM YOUR INTENTION

I give my body the gift of slumber.

Self-Care Principle # 17
Laugh to Live.

PONDER THIS

Did you know that laughter is one of the best things we can do for our bodies and our souls? Laughing has been shown to reduce stress, slow the aging process and improve other chronic health conditions.

PRACTICE SELF CARE

Laughter Yoga is a mindfulness activity that enhances breath, consciousness, and joy. You do not need to have a funny experience to reap the benefits of Laughter Yoga. Why? Because the body doesn't know the difference between a laugh triggered by humor and one that is self-induced. The benefits are the same. Try it! Just start laughing. You won't be able to stop and you'll feel great.

AFFIRM YOUR INTENTION

Ha…Ha…Ha-Ha-Ha!

Self-Care Principle # 18
Watch a Movie.

PONDER THIS

Comedy, tragedy, drama, sci-fi or scary? What's your pleasure?

PRACTICE SELF CARE

Need a little downtime? Curl up on the couch with a bowl of popcorn and click on that movie you've been meaning to watch, or perhaps one that you've seen 1000 times.

Laugh…cry…hide under a blanket…quote the lines. Sit back, relax, and enjoy a cinematic treat.

AFFIRM YOUR INTENTION

I deserve some downtime.

Self-Care Principle # 19
Get Out of the Zone.

PONDER THIS

Is your life plagued with routine? Do you engage in the same old thing day after day? Do you make it a habit to play it safe? Are you known as Mr./Ms. Dependable? While there is a time and place for everything, we grow when we put ourselves in situations that stretch us beyond our comfort zone. When life's experiences throw us curveballs, it's human nature to play it safe. But be careful, for "fear" will create a safe haven for mediocrity and a lackluster existence. The consequence? We lose out on the vitality of life.

PRACTICE SELF CARE

Let go of the status quo. Where in your life are you playing it safe? Get out of your own way. Find some small or big way to try something new. Take a calculated risk and enjoy the benefits that follow – creativity, innovation, unleashed inhibitions, and feelings of being powerful and courageous. Whatever it takes to view life through a new lens.

AFFIRM YOUR INTENTION

As I stretch myself beyond my comfort zone, I am creating an AMAZING life!

Self-Care Principle # 20
"Treat" Yourself.

PONDER THIS

Delicious, healthy food can nourish our being - physically, mentally, emotionally and spiritually. We hurry about our day, often taking the ritual of selecting, preparing, giving thanks and eating for granted. We don't think about how the food got here, how it is contributing to (or depleting) our body or how delightfully tasty it is. Food strengthens our temple and feeds our life force. Let's "treat" every step of this necessary but seemingly mundane routine with a joy-filled ceremony.

PRACTICE SELF CARE

Food Selection Ceremony
Grocery shopping can be a delight. Use this time to carefully select each ingredient. Look at the colors. Smell the fragrance. Think about how you will incorporate one item with another to create a delectable dish. Think about how happy and strong your body will be when it receives the food. Give thanks that you have the access and resources to be able to purchase food so easily. Finally, make your purchase with gratitude and reverence as you complete this ceremony.

Food Preparation Ceremony

The secret to really good food is love. When you cook with an intention, you find yourself focused on how you want it to taste, who will eat it, and how enjoyable the experience will be. Preparing or cooking food does take time but it does not have to be a long, drawn-out process. It's more about focus and concerted effort. Carve out a window of time. Now select all your ingredients with intentionality. Do research on recipes if necessary. Before you begin, decide if you want a little music. Turn on your favorite station so you can sing and dance as your cook. Prep your ingredients by washing, slicing, dicing, oiling pans, etc. Give thanks to the food for allowing you to partake of its essence. Begin the cooking process and enjoy. Finally, clean up with gratitude and reverence as you complete this ceremony.

Food Intake Ceremony

First, turn off all electronics and pay attention to your meal. Next, remember, our food is, or at least should be, a living species. As part of the cycle of life, the animal, fish, vegetables, fruits and herbs give their life so that we might be fed. Give thanks using this or another prayer: "Thank you Spirit for the food I am about to receive for the nourishment of my body. I thank all the ancestors, animals, fruits and vegetables so that I might be fed. I ask that I only absorb the nutrients and may everything else pass through me. Amen." Next, eat one bite at a time. Slowly chew your food. Savor every bite. Finally, if you are dining with someone, pay attention to the food and your partner(s). Have hearty conversations and laugh.

Finally, clean up with gratitude and reverence as you complete this ceremony.

AFFIRM YOUR INTENTION

I treat myself to wholesome foods.

TOOLS

DAY 1
PRINCIPLES OF SELF-MASTERY

Pre and Post 40-Day Journey Assessment Tools

Instructions: *Below you will find the Pre and Post 40-Day Journey Assessments. Read and answer each question by circling the number that corresponds to how consistently you practice the targeted Principle of Self-Mastery and Principle(s) of Self-Care. You should take the Pre Assessment on Day 0 and the Post Assessment on Day 41.*

Pre-40-Day Journey Assessment

How would you rate how consistently you practice the targeted *Principle of Self-Mastery* in your life?

| 1 | 2 | 3 | 4 | 5 | 6 | 7 | 8 | 9 | 10 |

Low   High

How would you rate how consistently you practice the targeted *Principle(s) of Self-Care* in your life?

| 1 | 2 | 3 | 4 | 5 | 6 | 7 | 8 | 9 | 10 |

Low   High

Post-40-Day Journey Assessment

How would you rate how consistently you practice the targeted *Principle of Self-Mastery* in your life?

| 1 | 2 | 3 | 4 | 5 | 6 | 7 | 8 | 9 | 10 |

Low   High

How would you rate how consistently you practice the targeted *Principle(s) of Self-Care* in your life?

| 1 | 2 | 3 | 4 | 5 | 6 | 7 | 8 | 9 | 10 |

Low   High

Faith Your Fear Reflection

Instructions: *After reading the Faith Your Fear section, write a reflection on how it relates to your life and experiences. Try to keep the focus of your comments on you rather than the role others may/may not have played. Remember, self-responsibility is a key to success.*

_____

_____

_____

_____

_____

_____

_____

_____

_____

_____

_____

_____

_____

_____

_____

_____

_____

DAY 2-7
PRINCIPLES OF SELF-MASTERY

CREATE YOUR WEEKLY PLAN

Instructions: *Create a plan for this week. The goal is to be consistent but realistic about what you can commit to. Keep in mind, though, that the more you practice the better you get at forming the new habit. Example: Principle of Self-Care activity is 10 deep breaths per day.*

Principles of Self-Mastery:

1. Referencing the steps in the *Activity to Form New Habits* section, identify what tasks/practices you will commit to this week to help you form your new habit. When or how often will you engage in them?

    _____

    _____

    _____

    _____

    _____

    _____

2. Referencing the selection of three affirmations for this principle, which will you recite three times per day this week?

    _____

    _____

    _____

    _____

Principles of Self-Care:

3. Referencing the *Activity to Form New Habits* section, decide how and when you will incorporate it into your week.

    _____

    _____

    _____

    _____

4. Reference the affirmation section and decide whether you will recite this one for the week or create your own. Write it below.

_____

_____

_____

_____

TRACK YOUR PROGRESS

Instructions: To track where you are on the journey, fill in the day of the week (Day 1, 2, 3, etc.). Color in 100% of the box if you fully met your commitment. Color in 50% of the box if you partially met your commitment. Leave the box empty on the days you did not meet your commitment at all.

	Day	Day	Day	Day	Day	Day	Day
Example Principle of Self-Care activity: *Breathe*							
Practice Your New Habit							
Affirmations(s)							
Principle of Self-Care Activity							

RATE YOUR STATE OF BEING THIS WEEK

Spiritual State of Being

Rate the level of your *Energy, Momentum and Strength of Character* for the week.

1	2	3	4	5	6	7	8	9	10

Low   High

Mental State of Being

Rate the quality of your *Thinking, Mindfulness and Consciousness* for the week

1	2	3	4	5	6	7	8	9	10

Low   High

Emotional State of Being

Rate the quality of your *Mood, Attitude and Enthusiasm* for the week.

1	2	3	4	5	6	7	8	9	10
Low									**High**

REFLECT ON YOUR PROGRESS

- What were your big and small wins? What changes are you noticing in yourself and/or your engagement with your environment or others?

_____

_____

_____

_____

_____

_____

_____

_____

- Where is there room for improvement? What commitment will you make to yourself?

_____

_____

_____

_____

_____

_____

_____

_____

I AM TRACEY KNIGHT
TAKE BACK...TRANSFORM...AND WIN AT YOUR OWN LIFE!

BIO

TRACEY KNIGHT
THE SELF-MASTERY COACH

"I AM Tracey Knight". Woman. Servant. Teacher. Mentor. A Powerful Feminine Leader. My purpose as a Self-Mastery Coach is to help men and women stretch their vision beyond the life they have, to achieve the life they want."

Coach Tracey Knight is an accomplished trainer, speaker, and certified life, career and personal empowerment coach. She has a no-nonsense approach to inspiring her clients to confront and change the beliefs and habits that prevent them from living an authentic and purpose-driven life.

Her signature *Self-Mastery Programs and Bootcamp* have been used by men and women, from baby boomers to millennials, as a means of addressing the perpetual fear of never achieving their full potential in the key areas of life - career, money, relationships and health. Her proprietary 4-stage method to self-mastery teaches individuals how to discover and reprogram the exhausting and self-defeating thoughts and habits that zap time, divert energy and impede success. Her live stream talk show, **You Revealed LIVE!** also serves as an inspiration to thousands of dedicated viewers who are reminded daily of their innate power to "Take Back, Transform and Win at Their Own Life."

Coach Tracey's prominence and success as a change agent is the result of her core belief, "I AM here to heal and serve humanity." This mantra drives her unrelenting persistence, compassion, and unwavering commitment to pay forward what has been given to her by her mother and life coach, Malane Shani.

Tracey Knight is a native of Cincinnati, Ohio but currently resides in Atlanta, Georgia. She holds a M. Ed. in Education Administration, a B.S. in Mathematics/Education and loves to cook, travel entertain family and friends. Tracey is also an avid dancer.

Made in the USA
Columbia, SC
15 November 2020